The Best of Bulletin Board

The Best of Bulletin Board

❦

Of Simple Pleasures,
Cute Kids, Dumb Customers,
The Kindness of Strangers,
and Other Scenes from the Human Comedy

PIONEER 🏛 BOOKS

ANDREWS AND McMEEL
A Universal Press Syndicate Company
Kansas City

Pioneer Books are published for the St. Paul Pioneer Press by Andrews and McMeel. Additional copies may be ordered by calling (800) 642-6480.

Library of Congress Cataloging-in-Publication Data

The Best of Bulletin board : of simple pleasures, cute kids, dumb
   customers, the kindness of strangers, and other scenes from the
   human comedy / [editor, Daniel Kelly].
      p.   cm.
   ISBN 0-8362-8060-1 : $8.95
      1. Anecdotes.   2. Bulletin boards.   I. Kelly, Daniel.
   II. Bulletin board (Saint Paul, Minn.)
   PN6261.B47   1994
   081—dc20   94-10855
                                                            CIP

PIONEER ⛰ BOOKS

The Best of Bulletin Board Editor: Daniel Kelly
Editorial Directors: Ken Doctor, David A. Fryxell
Promotion Director: Chris Oshikata
Design Director: Ellen Simonson

Cover design: George Diggs

CONTENTS

ৈ

FOREWORD

Editing Bulletin Board since its inception, in the spring of 1990, has been the most joyful experience of my working life. The readers of the St. Paul Pioneer Press—Bulletin Board's true creators—have, through their phone calls and letters and faxes, entertained and inspired in ways I could never have anticipated. I owe them more than I can say.

These are witty people, wise and tender, who have enriched their fellow readers by their simple willingness to tell the stories of their lives. They have laughed together and cried together—and, in so doing, they have created a new community for themselves. It's a friendly, comfortable, usually happy place—a refuge from the pinheads and the scoundrels who so often seem to have the upper hand.

Sometimes, Bulletin Board feels just like home. And if you're new here: Welcome!

After taking a second look at the nearly 1,500 Bulletin Boards that we've published over the past four years, I can say with no fear of contradiction that it was quite impossible to identify the "best." Too much good stuff; way too little space. What you'll find here, instead, is a small sampling of the contributions that seemed as fresh as when they first came my way. I hope you will find them to your liking.

I am in debt to a long list of colleagues at the Pioneer Press:

- Ken Doctor, now our managing editor, had the nerve to set aside a big block of space in our Express section when I proposed a half-formed notion without precedent in American newspapers: a column in which the readers could talk among themselves, day after day. I will be forever grateful for his confidence that I could make something valuable of that crazy idea.

- Features editors Dave Fryxell, Sue Campbell and Don Effenberger have given me every freedom to develop Bulletin Board as I saw fit.

- Copy editors Cheryl Burch-Schoff, Dana Davis, Bill Diehl, Beth Gauper, Phyllis Schuster, Becky Smith Welter and Jim Tarbox have saved me from innumerable gaffes.

- Reporter David Hawley has set aside his own work to take over Bulletin Board whenever I've been away, and he has kept Bulletin Board as lively as ever.

- Reporter Susan Barbieri brought a fresh eye to several chapters when my eyes were anything but fresh.

- Reporter Rick Shefchik's wit, enthusiasm and counsel have been nothing less than invaluable. He has been a true friend whenever I have needed one.

Finally, if you'll pardon the indulgence, I must thank my wife, Patty, and our daughters, Laura and Rose, who—without one word of complaint—went without a husband and father for many weeks while this collection came together. They have my love, always.

And now let me get out of the way.

Daniel Kelly

CHAPTER 1

The Best-Laid Plans . . .

Of fish and men: From **Gordy** of St. Paul:

"I want to tell you about a friend of mine—a red-haired, freckle-faced guy who'd blush at the drop of a hat. He wanted to get into sales, and it was suggested to him that he take a course in public speaking—to give himself a little more self-confidence. He took this course, and his first speech was gonna be on fishing.

"Well, he was scared to death, and he went to his class—and he was gonna have a visual antic in there to make it a little more humorous. What he did was: He went to the fish market and bought this big fish, and he was gonna finish his speech with '. . . and sometimes you *do* catch the one that got away'—and he was gonna cast out into the hallway from the classroom and have a friend of his hook the fish onto the line, and he was gonna reel it in.

"Well, his speech went a little shorter than he thought it would. The man went into the restroom, thinking that the speech was gonna go on for about 15 minutes. So my buddy tries to cast out into the hall. The first time, he misses. Second time he cast, he missed again; this time, the bobber hit the wall, and plastic splattered all over the class. The third time he cast out there, he made it—but the man was not outside. So he's saying '. . . and *sometimes* you . . . and *sometimes* you . . .'—and he realized the guy wasn't there, so he ran out, hooked the fish onto the line himself, ran back into the class, and said: 'Sometimes you *do* get the one that got away.'

"Well, he didn't think about the fact that a fish out of water would be much heavier than in water, and his line wasn't strong enough; he couldn't reel it in. The line snapped, and the line shot into the class and slapped some guy across the face, making a little red line. So my buddy ran out in the hall, picked up the fish, carried it in, and said: 'And sometimes you *do* get the one that got away.' And everyone was in hysterics—and he was so embarrassed. He was snickering, beet-red, trying to hold in the laughter—and he inadvertently went *knnnnnt* [sound of stifled laughter] and chuckled out his nose, emptying both nostrils onto the person in the front row—and ran out of that room, never to go back to that class."

". . . and sometimes you do catch the one that got away" (II): From **Mel** of Rogers:

"About 10 years ago, I had restored a 1958 23-foot Trojan, and I launched it in Medicine Lake at what wasn't a typical boat launch. It was a very steep hill going down.

"I had a Bronco four-wheel drive, and the boat was on a four-wheel trailer. I had to back the boat down this steep incline to get it to the water—and if anybody's ever backed up a four-wheel trailer, you realize it's a lot easier said than done.

"When I got the boat to the water, I couldn't quite get the Bronco close enough to the water. I had about three guys, and we unhooked the trailer from the Bronco and then pushed the trailer into the water a little bit. As soon as the boat started floating, it was OK—except that the trailer continued going underwater. Pretty soon, it was gone—because the underwater terrain was still about a 35-degree slope.

"So the boat was floating, and my Bronco was backed up to it—and no trailer. The trailer ended up about a hundred feet out into the lake. Bubbles were coming up.

"A friend of mine came by at the top of the hill there, looked down and saw the Bronco and no trailer, and he said: 'That's really a good trick. How did you do that?'

"I had to go get my scuba gear and dive into the lake; I found the trailer in about 35 feet of water—but my Bronco had wrecked the tranny coming back up the hill, so I tied about a hundred-foot rope to the tongue of the trailer underwater and then came up and tied the rope to the dock, underwater.

"I came back a week later, and some people were sitting around fishing. I didn't say anything; I just walked into the water about four feet, picked up the rope, which was tied about four feet deep onto the dock, backed my car up—and then, as they watched, I pulled this trailer out of 35 feet of water.

"I don't know what they thought."

"But [ribbit] officer! I'm not [ribbit] drunk!" From **Connie** of White Bear Lake:

"My daughter's high-school boyfriend, Bernie, was on his way home one rainy summer night when his car began to slip and slide. The road seemed alive. He stopped to check it out, and there were hundreds of frogs on the road.

"He didn't want to drive over them, so he found two paper sacks in his trunk and proceeded to fill the sacks with frogs, intending to release them in the pond near his house.

"A few miles down the road, the frogs started getting out of the bags and jumping all over—under his accelerator, in his hair, everywhere. In his attempt to get the frogs back in the sacks, he was weaving around on the road—and got stopped by a patrolman, who was certain that Bernie was drunk. Bernie protested and opened the car door, and there were frogs all over the place.

"The cop helped him empty the car and sent him home."

How to make a party bomb: canned ham! From **The Fabulous Scruffy Babe** of Hastings:

"I grew up in Birmingham, Michigan, which is sort of the Detroit-area equivalent of Edina. My parents both grew up pretty poor, so when they moved to Birmingham in 1970, they knew they had really 'made it.'

"They threw a lot of little dinner parties to get acquainted with the neighbors and to 'establish' themselves. My mother got really stressed over these little affairs. She was a wreck for days. Everything had to be perfect.

"At the most memorable dinner party, my mother decided to serve ham. She bought a canned ham. The directions on the can said something like 'You can cook this ham right in the can. Put in 350-degree oven for three hours. . . .' Either it didn't say anything about opening the can, or Mom didn't read that far.

"The party was going great. Everybody had a drink and some hors d'oeuvres. Then . . . BOOM! The can exploded, the oven door flew across the kitchen, and there was ham shrapnel everywhere. The story is only funny because no one was killed. *[BULLETIN BOARD NOTES: That would muffle the levity a bit, wouldn't it?]* We were picking ham off the walls for days."

Another fine mess: Here's a story you're not likely to see—alas—on "Northern Exposure," reported by **Joe** of Spring Valley, Wis.:

"In 1972, I was a schoolteacher in an Eskimo village in Alaska. At that time, most rural Alaskan villages didn't have running water and sewer. The village I lived in didn't, nor did most of the villages around it.

"A few villages away, there was a young, single teacher named Ed who lived in one of the prefab teacher houses often found near the schools at that time. Like most of us, Ed didn't have running water and sewer; he had a 55-gallon drum of water, and he had a honey bucket in his bathroom. A honey bucket was just a five-gallon steel bucket with a bail and handle and a toilet seat and lid on top of it. When it got full, you carried it outside and dumped it into the honey-bucket dump, which was sort of a septic tank that got pumped out every so often and then hauled away from the village and pumped into the tundra.

"Ed had a party one Friday night; had a bunch of teachers in, and of course everyone drank some beer—and the end result was that Ed's honey bucket got pretty full. At the end of the party, he went to sleep. Woke up the next morning with probably a mild hangover and couldn't face emptying his honey bucket, which was full to the brim. Besides that, he had to go to town for Saturday and Sunday, to do some visiting and shopping. I should add that it was quite cold at the time, and cold for rural Alaska means real cold.

"So Ed hopped on his snowmobile and headed off 60 miles to town to buy groceries and supplies. Got back late Sunday night, opened his prefab-house door, and immediately realized that his oil stove had gone out because he'd neglected to pump oil into his oil tank before he left. Of course, his 55-gallon drum of water was frozen up—and so, unfortunately, was his honey bucket. He decided that he would face that in the morning.

"I think he probably slept at a neighbor's, but anyway: Came in in the morning, got his honey bucket out, re-ignited his oil stove—so he had heat, but he couldn't dump his honey bucket because it was frozen solid. So he had a great idea: Ed put his honey bucket on the oil stove; he knew in just a few minutes, it would warm up and he could dump it.

"Unfortunately, he went off to school, to his first class, and forgot his honey bucket on the stove.

"At 10 o'clock, he came home for coffee. He opened the door to his house, and an amazing odor hit him in the face. His honey bucket had been boiling on his oil stove for an hour and a half.

"I don't remember what Ed did next; he may have left the village for good."

Classical gas: Here's **The Music Man** of St. Paul, with an account he titled "A Night at the Opera":

"T.G.I.F.—and it's not just any Friday; it's a Minnesota Orchestra Friday.

"The evening begins uneventfully enough: home from work, dinner, a little TV, get ready to go to Orchestra Hall, drive there.

"We always park in a surface lot a block away. It's one of those where you put the money in an envelope in a little locked box, under threat of being towed if they come by and find you haven't paid. We've done this routine a zillion times at the same lot.

"This time, there's a guy standing out there saying we're supposed to pay *him*, not the box. He has no uniform, no badge, no credentials. What's more, he's standing right next to a sign posted in the lot that reads: 'PAY THE BOX ONLY. NO ATTENDANT ON DUTY.'

"After I park, he asks for my money. I ask how I'm supposed to know he really works there.

"His response: 'Would I be standing out here in the cold if I didn't *have* to be here?'

"My unspoken thought: 'Well, if a constant stream of strangers were handing you cash . . . *yes*, perhaps you might!'

"At the risk of hurting his feelings, I paid the box instead of him. I will be left forever wondering whether he really was supposed to be there or not.

"Leaving this little life-adventure behind, we go on to Orchestra Hall—and promptly realize we left the tickets at home, 10 miles back.

"My first thought is: Maybe somebody at home can fax the tickets to a fax machine at the theater. This plan is quickly vetoed by my wife, who points out that a) we don't have a fax machine at home; b) there's nobody left at home except the dog; and c) faxing skills were not covered in canine-obedience school.

"We decide, instead, to plead for mercy at the box office. I feel guilty asking for a level of trust that I just denied the parking-lot guy. I can imagine them asking: 'How do we know you really bought tickets?'

"But they are unbelievably nice about it, getting their computer to print out a pair of replacement tickets in about 30 seconds—without even a service fee, such as one might expect to be asked to cough up (or: up with which one might expect to cough). Many thanks, Minnesota Orchestra.

"We find our seats—which, while not exactly opening vistas on the interior of the hall, do open vistas of new meaning on the term 'partial-view seating.'

"We are surrounded by an interesting cast of characters:

"To my right is a young man who is apparently committed to the setting free of bodily odors. 'Hygienically liberated,' one might say. My wife has generously given me the seat closer to him. I consider trying to expel posterior breezes his way—because, you know: When in aroma, do as the aromans do. I decide against escalating this battle, fearing what else might be in the adversary's arsenal.

"To our left is a woman who immediately begins telling my wife about the panic attacks she gets sitting this close (second row) to the edge of the side balcony. My wife wants us to scoot our movable chairs to the right, to give this anxiety-ridden woman a little more room. I decline, fearing asphyxiation.

"In front of me is a woman who, throughout the concert, engages in what my biology professors used to refer to as a 'fixed action pattern'—perhaps genetically ingrained and irrepressible: Cough a few times, open purse, noisily unwrap ineffective cough drop, close purse, move chair, flip through program, talk to companion, cough. Repeat.

"In front of my wife is a man who has been ordering too many of those 1970s retrospective music tapes. His shirt is literally unbuttoned to his navel. No undershirt. To emphasize the point, he occasionally scratches his chest hairs, carefully in time with the music.

"The centerpiece of the concert is the much-ballyhooed world premiere of a new violin concerto by John Adams. Unfortunately, it appears that the work has been pushed onto the concert schedule a bit too soon; the composer hasn't yet gotten around to putting in the melody. Despite this flaw, the audience applauds wildly—perhaps trying to tell Mr. Adams: 'You finish that piece up with a good tune, and you'll really have something there.'

"Wild applause is supposed to bring the composer onto the stage. But it doesn't.

"The concert concludes with a Brahms symphony. Man, oh man, you can't beat that. No matter what has gone before, you always get your money's worth with Brahms on the program. It is marred only by Mr. Odor Outer pulling out—I kid you not—a complete orchestral score and conducting along with Edo de Waart.

"Wild applause again fails to bring out the composer.

"Back at the car, I notice the parking lot looking somewhat deserted. Did everybody else just leave before us, or did the towing companies have a heyday?

"On the trip home, I notice the car has suddenly developed a nasty, scary shimmy at highway speeds.

"Perhaps I should have paid the young man, after all."

CHAPTER 2

The Simple Pleasures

Bulletin Board has been rich with reports of life's easy comforts since this call, in August of 1992, from a young lady named **Brooke** *of Blaine, who gave us the words:*

"Today my friend and I were talking about simple pleasures, and I realized that one of the simplest pleasures and most wonderful things is the sound of rain when you're going to bed. It's just so comforting to hear the rain go pitter-patter against the window."

John of St. Paul: "Years ago, I used to spend time at my aunt and uncle's farm. The farmhouse was a two-story house. Many warm summer evenings, as I lay in bed upstairs, I could hear at a very faraway distance the sound of a steam-locomotive train whistle. I'll never forget that sound—so lonesome and so forlorn, and yet so relaxing that it put me to sleep many a night. Those were the good old days."

Auntie Love of Maplewood: "Peeling off a sunburn and hearing the ripping sound it makes. It's wonderful."

Peggy of Shoreview: "Tonight, we visited someone in the hospital who just had a little baby, and one of the gifts was a picture frame wrapped in that plastic bubble wrap—and I *really* enjoy poppin' those little plastic bubble-wrap poppers."

Jackie of the East Side: "Being a hockey mom for 10 years now, with at least that many still to go, I realized that at 6:30 on weekend mornings in a cold, damp arena, there is nothing that compares to the sight and sound of your son gracefully flying down the ice. The crisp, cutting sound of skates into a clean sheet of ice is wonderful. Call me crazy!"

Anonymous woman of Macalester-Groveland: "I love—absolutely love—to be the first person to open that jar of creamy peanut butter—and *stick* the knife in. But I've got three kids, and lately I don't get to do it very often."

Dixie of Lowertown: "A simple pleasure: when you go to a fast-food place

7

and get your basic burger-and-fries, and you eat your burger-and-fries, and then you reach down into the bag and find just those last couple long, yummy french fries at the bottom of the bag."

Eric of Maplewood: "One of my simple pleasures is when you're opening a Band-Aid—and the red string cuts perfectly down the side of the wrapper."

Tim of Mendota Heights: "After you do a bunch of towels in the dryer and you're cleanin' off that lint trap—I love peelin' off that big old pile of lint."

Larry of Hugo: "While sorting the laundry last night as it came out of the dryer, I experienced one of life's simple pleasures. All of my socks had mates."

Lynn of Oakdale: "After you finish painting a wall, pulling the masking tape off the baseboard and trim and seeing a perfect bead of paint right along the edge—now, *that's* nice."

Jane of St. Paul: "When my hair is quite dirty, and it's being lathered and washed by an attendant in the beauty shop, and when it's rinsed, it goes squeak, squeak, squeak. That squeaky sound is wonderful."

Shoney of White Bear Lake: "The *ker-plink* you hear after you've canned food and take it out of the boiling-water bath. You set it aside in the cool air, and the lids go *ker-plink.*"

Dave of Minneapolis: "Lighting the pilot on my gas oven. I love the *whoosh* sound as the gas is ignited and the match is extinguished. There's also that little thrill of knowing that the gas has been lit without anything blowing up."

Ruth of St. Paul likes to "vacuum near a door, and you can hear the clinking of tiny bits of gravel going into the vacuum cleaner. It really makes you feel like you're accomplishing something."

Ann of St. Paul: "A simple pleasure, for me, is using my vacuum after Christmas, when I've been vacuuming up pine needles and the whole house starts smelling like pine trees again, like Christmas. I try to keep that bag in there as long as I can, so that I can keep smelling it as long as I can into the new year."

Anonymous woman: "I have a simple pleasure—especially for little children who just had to get glasses. If you're very nearsighted, you can take your glasses off to look at the Christmas tree—and the lights get very big and soft. It's beautiful."

Sally of White Bear Lake: "My sister is married to a doctor, and a few years ago, I told her that I wanted a stethoscope for my birthday. She got one for me—and ever since, one of my simplest pleasures has been lying in bed listening to my stomach growl. There's a lot more going on down there than you think. It's also kinda fun to put it on someone else's throat and listen to them swallow."

Effie of Austin: "My simple pleasure in the fall is popping all the acorns as I ride my bike in the street."

J.Z. of Roseville: "Finding golf balls on a golf course. In my memory are some lovely, brisk late-fall days when golfers had deserted the links—my dog romping, and I tromping through the rough at the edge of the golf course. I'd go home with a few golf balls and a tired and happy dog."

Axman of Mondovi, Wis.: "A simple wood-splitting pleasure: to take a swing with the maul at a block over a foot thick that looks as if it might require three or four blows to split, and to feel that perfect pop of a centered hit and see the block leap apart into two neat half-cylinders, clean and aromatic, rocking gently on either side of the chopping block.

"All who wish to experience this pleasure for themselves are welcome to come to my woodpile and try it. Wood, maul and instruction provided."

Ardathian Fields of St. Paul: "My simple pleasure: when it rains really hard and you're walking out of work and it's done raining and there's a puddle of water on the parking lot and, in the water, blue sky and white fluffy clouds are reflected, making a black parking lot into a piece of the sky."

Robyn of Maplewood: "My husband told me the other day, as we were driving down the freeway in the rain, that his most favorite simple pleasure is to drive under a bridge—and the rain stops, and then when you drive past the bridge, it starts hitting your windshield again. He loves that."

Merlyn of St. Paul: "Yesterday, I was driving the Suzuki Death Car down Marshall Avenue. I was just going to cross the Lake Street Bridge into Minneapolis, and I saw this gigantic puddle at the bottom of the hill. There was nobody around, so I wasn't gonna splash anybody—and I just *blasted* into it. It was like surfing; the water went up over my car, and I had to turn my wipers on. It was great!"

The Rainbow Warrior of St. Paul: "Today at suppertime, there was a rainstorm—a little bit of a downpour, with the sun shining off to the west, and there was a double rainbow off to the east, and it was quite beautiful. And then tonight, I walked outside with my dog, and I see the Northern Lights shining. Right now, I have $4 in my pocket to last until my next payday, but from what I've gotten today, with the rainbow and the Northern Lights, I feel like a rich woman."

Kroz of Winona: "One of the biggest, simplest pleasures is when you're taking your finals and you fill in that last circle, and you know it's time to go home."

Kristy of Lake Elmo: "When you're hitting crab apples with a baseball bat and you hit one just right and it splatters all over the place and the juice sprays down on you. That is really cool."

Betty of White Bear Lake: "My simple pleasure is knowing that after the first good snowfall, my yard looks as good as everyone else's."

Bob of St. Paul: "You can't beat it: sitting in a hot bath, expecting snow, drinking café latté and doing the crossword puzzle. That's the best."

Elizabeth Stokes of Apple Valley: "I'm 7 years old, and my simple pleasure is to go over and cuddle up on the heat vent with my blanket on a cold winter day."

Linda of St. Paul: "I was walking through the house, shutting off the lights—and I realized, when the last light was off, that it was still light in the house—because of the reflection from the snow. Wintertime snow makes sort of a natural night light. I like that."

The Booner of Grey Cloud Island: "I work nights. I get off work usually about 1:15, 1:30. And when there's a new snowfall, I absolutely love being the first vehicle cruisin' down the back roads through the virgin snow."

Lady Cheesehead: "I'm a middle-aged, conservative-type woman, and I drive an older car. My simple pleasure is being one of the first ones to go into our parking lot at work after a light little snow, when no one else has driven out on it. I like to just drive out there and whip a few s— ties . . . whoops! Can I say that? [BULLETIN BOARD NOTES: Well, not exactly. You could have said 360s, U'ies, Louies, Doughnuts, Brodies—any number of things. But you didn't, did you?] Well, you know what I mean—just spin around a little bit.

"And later on, when we're in work, you can hear some of 'em talk and mention the tracks, and they say: 'Oh, some kid here must've had fun this morning.'

"And I just sit there and not say anything and just think: 'Yes, I did.' "

Carl of Superior, Wis.: "The cold snap brought back one of my simple pleasures—which is to go outside in the morning, crank up my sits-outside, never-plugged-in '72 Chevy pickup, and use it to jump-start all the nice, new cars of my neighbors."

Anonymous man of Highland Park: "One of my simple pleasures: being out in this beautiful, fluffy snow and quietly slipping over to the neighbors'— who are an older couple—and shoveling their steps and sidewalks without them knowing it.

"They'll come home and see that it's been done for them—and that'll hopefully give them a simple pleasure of their own."

Katherine and Paul of Sunfish Lake: "One of our simple pleasures is running around the house with a golf club and knocking off all of the icicles that hang down from the roof."

Brett of White Bear Lake: "In the middle of winter, me and my friends like to drive down to the Dairy Queen in the Midway, sit in the car with the heat on and eat really cold ice cream. Pretend it's summer, or something."

Nancy on Niles of St. Paul, after watering her plants in the depth of winter: "I held my hand underneath and let the water drip through, and it felt just like rain—and then I could smell this wonderful, wet, earthy smell, and it just reminded me of spring. I *know* spring is coming."

Norma of Northfield: "To step out in the morning after God has washed the world and smell the wonderful lilacs."

June Zimmerman of Blaine: "Long ago, I tried to start a little herb patch on the edge of my lawn. It didn't work out. But now, about every third time I mow, I hit some dill that has valiantly tried to come up. Mmmm, that smells good."

Computer Kevin of parts hereabouts: "I was walking through one of the county parks. Somehow I got off the beaten track, and I was walking through a dark part of the woods. Came upon this little clearing, bright sunlight streaming down. Went over to middle of the clearing and sat down. Beautiful early-summer day. And I noticed that in this little clearing—25 feet across, or so—were all kinds of strawberries flowering. Wild strawberries. I just sat there—and boy, you could breathe in the scent of the strawberries, and the sunshine, and the cool breeze—and every time I get hyper or stressed out, I just sit back and close my eyes and think of sitting in that little glade, in the sunlight, surrounded by strawberries."

Sue of the East Side: "I love the smell of fresh, new rubber. I think it comes from getting new dolls every Christmas when I was a girl. I think that's why it smells so good and makes me think of happy times."

Kris of St. Paul: "I'm calling with my simple pleasure. I can't believe I actually have time. I'm the mother of two; one is 2½, and the other is 7 months. My simple pleasure is when I can, by some miracle, get them both to sleep at the same time in the afternoon—and it's actually quiet enough in my house for me to hear my clock tick."

Jill of Roseville: "As the mother of a 5-year-old, a 2-year-old and a 3-month-old, I find most days filled with simple pleasures—but when the kids and I are having one of *those* days, we have one simple pleasure in common: the sound of Daddy's truck pulling into the driveway after work."

Paula of St. Paul: "When my three little boys were little babies and would have a stuffy nose but couldn't really blow it successfully, we'd need to help out by rolling a piece of Kleenex into a point to push up into a nostril, to dig it out. And if you're lucky, you might get a real big offering—and feel pretty proud of yourself! And secondly: You know when you have a tickle in your ear and you stick your finger in to scratch, when you pull out your fingernail and find that you've got a big hunk of dark wax? That's pretty satisfying, too."

Andrea and Ben's Mom (echoed by **Nancy** of South St. Paul and **Pam** of Apple Valley): "I think the greatest joy of parenthood is rocking in your arms a freshly bathed, sweet-smelling baby, having them look into your eyes as they are gently falling off to sleep."

Julie P. of South St. Paul: "To walk by the baby monitor and hear my little darling girl breathe."

Laurie of Frederick, Wis.: "My 9-month-old son learned how to clap his hands yesterday, and when I walked into his room this morning, he was standing up in his crib. He got a big smile on his face, and he started to clap. *Nothing* beats applause and a standing ovation from your baby."

Freshman of Eagan: "My mama has the flu, and along with feeling horrible, she has all the other symptoms—like the chills. So my simple pleasure is washing and drying her sheets and putting 'em on her bed really warm, so when she gets in her bed from off the couch, she's really warm, and she doesn't have the chills anymore."

Theresa of Maplewood: "My simple pleasure is: after negotiating and arguing and fighting all day with my two young sons and then fighting with them at night to try to get them to bed and asleep, going into their rooms and looking at their little angel faces sleeping away, drooling all over the sheets."

Heidi of Woodbury: "Smelling my husband's cologne on the kids after he's hugged and kissed them good-bye for the day."

Suzanne of Merriam Park: "My simple pleasure is watching my 4-month-old daughter sleep on my husband's chest and seeing how much alike they look. It's really neat to watch."

Laurie of St. Paul: "Here's a simple pleasure I'm realizing right now. My 2-year-old son is sitting on his grandpa's lap (he was named after his grandpa); the two of them are watching the Discovery channel together, and my father is explaining the Egyptian monuments to him. That's a simple pleasure: that I can watch my son learn from my father."

Bullet Dodger of Frogtown: "The peace and quiet that breaks out when you shut the TV off."

Guinevere of Afton: "I have a simple pleasure I'd like to reveal. After I get up in the morning, feed the kids breakfast, clean up after breakfast, get the kids dressed, pack their school lunches, pack their school bags and finally shove them out the door to the bus, then the Nintendo machine is all mine. I can play it all by myself—and you know what? I'm almost as good at Nintendo as they are."

Judy of Blaine: "A simple pleasure for me: Working hard all day, and being tired, and coming home—and my pet cockatiel gives me a wolf whistle and says 'Hello, baby.' "

Theresa of St. Paul: "I've worn contacts for about 15 years, and my simple pleasure is taking my lenses out at the end of the day and rubbing the heck out of my eyes."

Mars of Luck, Wis.: "It's been a long day, and I've had the same ugly boots on all day. I come home and sit back in the big chair and take the boots off—and then I reach down and have to peel the socks from the bottom of my feet. It's just great. It's ideal. Dramatic.

"I'm thinking there might be an invention in there, too—like some sort of a Teflon sock. Maybe not."

Spock of Minneapolis: "My wife exclaims every night when she takes off her bra what a simple pleasure it is, what a joy it is."

Kathy of Forest Lake: "My greatest simple pleasure is when I hear my husband say those three little words that I long to hear: 'Let's eat out.' "

Cool of Oakdale: "On a hot summer day, lying on my bed, spreading my legs, and letting the fan cool wherever it may."

River Rat of Indian Point: "One of my simple pleasures is to sit in our screen porch and watch the mosquitoes try to get in."

Anonymous woman: "I've had a slow drain in my bathroom sink for about three months—you know, where it fills up with water and then it takes about 15 minutes to drain out. I've put in Drano and all this other stuff. So today I just went crazy and stuck a hanger down this sink—and pulled up a hair ball about the size of a mouse. I'm pretty excited, because now the water drains right away."

Sue's Oldest Daughter of Woodbury: "My mom's simple pleasure is opening and closing doors after you apply oil to the hinges."

Nancy of Altoona, Wis.: "My 2-year-old son Aaron's simple pleasure is riding over rumble strips on the road. He just sits in his car seat and squeals."

Hippie of South St. Paul: "My simple pleasure is: Now that my boyfriend's in jail, I actually do know where he is."

Cookie of Marine: "We've got a 15-pound, 9½-month-old cat—and when he comes into our waterbed at night, it's like having the Magic Fingers mattress at the motel, only you don't have to plug in quarters. It's heaven."

Jo of St. Paul: "After my cat has gone berserk until I let him out, he comes back in the door and *stretches . . . out . . .* one leg at a time. He just looks so wonderful as he's stretching in pure pleasure at the comfort of the house."

Dennis of the West Side: "One of my simple pleasures is putting whipped cream between my toes and letting my cats lick it out. It's the greatest." (**Green Henry** of White Bear Lake: "My brother Ray and I were wondering how Dennis could possibly *discover* how pleasureful that was. I mean: You don't just walk around and put whipped cream in between your toes—I would think *especially* with cats around the house.")

Karen Gomez of St. Paul: "We used to get up on Saturday morning, and my dad would make waffles—and we'd stick the leftover waffles between our toes. Waffles work better than whipped cream, because you can grab 'em with your toes, and the dog has to chew on your toes a little bit to get those waffles out. That was always fun."

Mike of St. Paul: "I like picking the toe-jam dirt out of the corners of my big toes."

Jay of St. Paul: "One of my simple pleasures is when you're eating potato chips or Cheetos, and you know how it just gets caked up in your teeth? And you just want to pick it out so bad? Well, I like it when there's like a little knobby sticking over the edge of your tooth, and you can just gnaw at it with your tongue and try to chisel it out with your tongue and get it all loose, and then it falls out so you don't have to pick it out with your fingers. Yep, that's a simple pleasure for you."

Scot of White Bear Lake: "I had my jaw wired shut for six weeks—and the biggest thing I missed was licking my lips. You never know what a great thing it is to be able to lick your lips. It's truly an awesome pleasure."

Kay of Star Prairie: "As the proverbial little old lady, I have experienced most of life's pleasures, both simple and otherwise.

"My failing eyesight has dimmed some of the joy, but I must tell you of the great satisfaction I receive when I can guide my tweezers to that unseen chin whisker and yank that sucker out."

Mary of Rosemount: "My simplest pleasure is in the morning, when I awake. Only people who have a hearing problem will understand this. When I go to sleep at night, I take off my hearing aids; I don't hear anything, not even the telephone ringing. When I wake up in the morning, in the summer, I put my hearing aids on, and I can hear the birds outside my window. That's a real pleasure."

Jenny of St. Paul: "One of my greatest simple pleasures is when the last song that I hear in the car before work—the one that sticks in my mind forever—is some song that I actually like."

Analiese of White Bear Lake: "I'm just sitting here listening to my favorite tape. This is a tape I bring everywhere—to Grandma's for the weekend, to the beach (during beach months, of course) and even to school for in my locker, so I can catch 30 seconds or so between classes. My simple pleasure is that when I'm listening to my special tape, not only do I know what song is next, I also know the exact length of the pause between songs and the exact pitch of the first note of the next song—so I can start in singing right on beat one. Elemental mirth."

Chickadee-dee-dee-dee-dee of St. Paul: "I just love afternoon naps. It has to be in the sunshine, and preferably with the window open, and the air has to be very fresh. What I like the best is when I can *feel* myself falling asleep, and I just sink deeper and deeper. It's a delicious, voluptuous, wonderful feeling."

Elaine of Little Falls (echoed by **Laurie** of St. Paul): "My simple pleasure is crawling into a bed with sheets fresh off the wash line. You can still smell the wind in them." (**Susan P.** of Cathedral Hill had another view of smelling wind in sheets: "Reminded me of my ex-husband—and another swell reason to be glad I'm single.")

Debbie of Inver Grove Heights: "The best thing is sleeping in clean sheets with freshly shaven legs."

The Clover Kicker: "This works any time of year, but especially during the fall and winter—and even more so with flannel sheets, as opposed to cotton. When you climb into bed, leave your socks on. After you and the bed are sufficiently warmed up, slip off the socks. The feeling is terrific. It works even better if you've slipped off into that limbo state between full wakefulness and deep sleep, but it takes an acute sense of timing to do that consistently. Once I'm gone, I'm *really* gone. On the other hand, once the socks come off, insomnia doesn't have a chance."

Mary of Vadnais Heights: "A simple pleasure: It's when you wake up at night, and you're not sure what time it is, and you're about to glance over at the clock—hoping it doesn't say 6:29, when you know the alarm rings at 6:30—and when you look, it's only about 1:45 or something, and you get to snuggle back under the covers."

Tanya of St. Paul: "One simple pleasure: the point in the morning when you wake after a night of tossing and turning and thinking you'll *never* fall asleep."

Carol of South Minneapolis: "Turning off the alarm clock on Friday, savoring the fact that I don't have to hear it for two days."

Ardis of St. Cloud: "Lying in bed and listening to my husband grinding the coffee beans for our morning coffee."

Tanna of Centuria, Wis., with a pair: "The first one: You have to get up real early in the morning, and it has to be very quiet, but sometimes I can hear the sound that the sugar makes when it goes into my coffee. That's a precious one, because it's not always quiet enough for me to hear that. The second one is the sound that sharp scissors make when they're cutting through fabric. Nothing like it."

Corey of Woodbury: "I'm fortunate to have a couple of acres out here in Woodbury. The back of the yard goes up to a big hill—and this is one of life's best simple pleasures:

"Got up about 7 o'clock. Went downstairs to make myself a cup of coffee. The east sky, behind the hill, was just starting to get a little bit light. All of a sudden, I saw them: three beautiful deer. Turned off the light real quickly and just sat there and stared for five minutes.

"What a terrific way to start the day."

Poet Past of Minneapolis: "When you're watching 'Jeopardy!' and nobody knows the answer—and you do! And you scream and yell at them."

Jennifer of Inver Grove Heights: "One thing that makes me very happy, for some strange reason, is when I'm in line at the grocery store, at work—or anywhere—and I see hairs from someone's head on their sweater or shirt. I just love to pick them off until the shirt is all clean and looks good."

The Assistant Editor of Forest Lake: "I have one of those big calendar blotters on my desk at work—you know, one of those big old things that covers the desk's whole writing surface, and you tear off a fresh sheet each month. What a pleasure that is—to peel off the torn, stained top page when the old month is over and have a fresh, unspoiled month underneath. What I hate is when I go to peel off that old top sheet and find that the coffee I spilled yesterday has soaked through, wrinkling the new month and ruining that pristine beauty. It's kinda like finding a candy wrapper when you're way off in the wilderness."

Bigfoot of Cottage Grove: "I love to get a batch of newly printed checks from the bank—and then you get that new, pristine-white check register. It always looks so nice before I start writing in it with different colors of ink, and making mathematical mistakes that I have to correct, and just totally screwing the whole thing up."

Michelle of St. Paul: "My simple pleasure is when my checkbook balances—to the exact penny. Such a great feeling."

Bill of Oakdale: "My simple pleasure is to see signal lights turn from green to yellow when I'm in the *middle* of the intersection, knowing that I'll make it across, free and clear. I then scream: 'Yeeeeee-hah!' Blue skies!"

Hatless of Hastings: "You're driving down the highway. You spot a police patrol car in your rear-view mirror. You glance at your speedometer. You're doing exactly 55. Feels gooooood."

Kate of Eagan: "I just wanted to tell you the best thing that has ever happened in my life. You know, you're driving down 35W or 494, and a guy gets behind you who's goin' about 8,000 miles an hour, and he puts the brights on, you know, because he really wants to pass you. You say 'Fine'—after, you know, half an hour, 45 minutes. And you get out of the guy's way, he tears off at 120, and about five minutes down the road, you see him pulled over. The cherries are goin'; the cop is goin', 'Sir, can I please see your license?' It is such a beautiful experience. If you can, kids, give it a try."

Juin of St. Paul: "I remember, when I was growing up, going to the library and being allowed to sit there amid all the dusty old books for *hours* on end. You could just learn anything about the entire universe, just sitting there. So my simple pleasure now is—even though I usually take my four kids to the library every couple weeks—my simple pleasure is the day when I can go over there by myself, sit on the floor, and just look at the books by myself."

Chris of Highland Park: "A great simple pleasure: when you put on new guitar strings. There's nothing like new strings on a guitar; you cannot put it down. It feels so good that you just keep playing it and playing it and playing it. And strings are very cheap; they're only $3.95, and that makes 'em a really good simple pleasure."

The Piano Man of St. Paul: "A simple pleasure: when I haven't played piano in a few days, and I finally get a chance to sit down, and I finally start playing the keys, and my fingers just sink right in. It feels so great."

Pat of St. Paul: "My simple pleasure is preparing beets. I put 'em in a pressure cooker—and after they cook and have a chance to cool off, you get to enjoy one of the most sensual experiences in the whole world of cooking: taking the outside skin off the beet. What you do is: You take that little stem part off, and you hold the beet in your hand and just give a little bit of a squeeze, and the beet underneath plops out into your other hand, all shiny and red and warm. It's just the most wonderful feeling—and if you haven't tried it, believe me that it's a whole lot more fun than just opening up a can."

Dick of Lowertown: "When I was a kid, growing up on a farm, I always thought one of the neatest things was to be cultivating corn or soybeans all day—and at the end of the day, driving home and going by all the lovely green rows of soybeans or corn, surrounded by black, black, black dirt. A wonderful feeling. Green rows and black dirt."

Mike of Fridley: "My grandpa's place had about a 20-acre peat bog, and it was the most prolific producer of fireflies I've ever seen on the face of the Earth. It was a real kick to watch them come rising up out of the bog at their pre-appointed time each night. No fireworks show could rival that."

Linda of St. Paul: "One of my simple pleasures is to return home after a night class and see three pairs of tennis shoes lined up at the door. It's in that instant that I know my kids are all home safe and sound in bed, and Dad's asleep in his recliner."

Andrea of Circle Pines: "Watching my kindergartner tie his own shoes."

Joel of Redwood Falls: "I get a kick out of watching little kids walk. It's so neat the way they flip-flop their feet and swing their arms back and forth."

P.B. of St. Paul: "I like to be really hungry and then drink really cold water—and feel the cold water just goin' down my esophagus. You can feel it just goin' down right behind your breastbone, and then it just kinda sets in your stomach. Really cool!"

Julie of Gopher Prairie: "I keep a list of simple pleasures in my journal. I just love 'em. I write down everything I see that makes me the least little bit happy. Then I read it when I think: 'Hey, you know, life really stinks.' I look at all the things that make me happy, and I think: 'Things aren't so bad.' "

Raven of White Bear Lake: "To all of the people who know how to find the simple pleasures: You have found the magic secret of life."

CHAPTER 3

Where Have You Gone, Mrs. Malaprop?

Oh, she's out there, all right:

Bernie of Inver Grove Heights: "My dear wife—who I love, of course—constantly comes up with things that I can't help but chuckle at.

"Today, she was telling me that there was something she keeps forgetting to do. She says: 'I don't know what's wrong. Things just seem to go in one brain and out the other.' "

Judy of Bayport: "My former roommate Jude used to say: 'I could do that with both eyes tied behind my back.' "

Tim of Highland Park: "My wife just said to me: 'That's the blind calling the kettle black.' "

Susan H. of Spring Valley, Wis.: "At a family gathering, my oldest sister was describing a serious health problem plaguing her in-laws. She said: 'It's really a sad kettle of worms.' "

The Forensic Ornithologist of Winona: "A lady I worked with years ago had been involved with a group making elaborate plans for a holiday party at work—and one by one, her helpmates dropped by the wayside and left her to bear the burden.

"She was bemoaning that fact one day to me, and she said: 'Well, wouldn't you know it? They left me standing there, holding Pandora's bag of worms.' "

The Transplanted St. Paulite of Spring Park: "At a seminar I attended last week, the woman running it was saying there were some flaws in a plan—some 'kinks in the ointment.' "

The PR Hack of White Bear Lake: "A friend was grousing the other day about a co-worker with a track record of rocking the boat unnecessarily.

19

With an exasperated sigh, my friend threw up her hands and said: 'The guy is always throwing wrenches in the ointment.' "

Debbie of Inver Grove Heights: "I was in a meeting the other day, and one of the women said: 'Well, that went over like a lead potato.' "

Nancy of St. Paul: "The other day, my boyfriend was talking about some guy who he thinks is making a lot of money. He said: 'Boy, he must be raking it in hand over foot.' "

Sweetheart of St. Paul: "The husband of one of my daughters was quite worried about something. She said he was waiting for the other foot to drop."

Linda of Falcon Heights: "I was in a meeting today, and a co-worker said: 'You better be careful. You're walking on thin water.' "

The Mongolian Stomper of the East Side: "We were up ice-fishing, me and my friend Spanky. He's got this sonar that shows, in orange, when fish are down there. I told him I had to go take a leak, and he said: 'Don't go now. It's lit up like a racehorse.'

"So I told him: 'Well, let me know when the lights go off. I've gotta go out and pee like a Christmas tree.' "

Beagle of Stillwater: "A few weeks ago, in my physics class, a friend and I were working on a nasty problem. Finally, he came up with a relevant equation and said: 'Pull that out of your hat and smoke it!' "

Diz of Ham Lake: "I work in a bank, and last night, one of our customers called and asked me to take a look at his account, because he had gotten a notice of insignificant funds."

Debra of Inver Grove Heights: "I only report this with much affection for a co-worker whom I dearly love and who makes going to work every day a true pleasure. She was having some trouble with one department and had had it up to here, and she had to get in touch with the manager. She comes storming around the corner and asks: 'Who's the big head cheese?' "

Mary of West St. Paul: "My friend Beth and I were talking at lunch the other day—a very heated discussion about why Personnel is moving so slowly on a situation. Beth reassured me that they were moving slowly because they wanted to make sure all their nuts were in one bolt."

Hank of St. Paul: "One of the managers came in to give us a pep talk and tell us how proud of all of us he was—and he wanted to point out one person in particular. I'll call her Mary Brown. So he comes in, and he says: 'I want to thank you all for what a great job you're doing. The way that you all are working, I think we can say that this is really an efficient machine we're experiencing here.'

"And then he points to Mary Brown and says: 'And here is the main clog.' "

M.C. of Shoreview: "We had a president of our company, and every time he would see a competitor's new product in a magazine, he would always say: 'Boy, they're gonna eat our clock with that one.' "

P.J. of Burnsville: "Yesterday, I was talking to one of my fellow workers about an upcoming project and how everything had to be in order for the project to go smoothly. His final words were: 'We need to make sure all our eggs are in a row.' "

Carmen of Stillwater: "The other day, I heard the guy who sits near my work station say to a customer: 'That puts the egg before the cart—or is that "the cart before the egg"?' "

S.A.W. of St. Paul: "The other day, my younger sister Charlotte was describing someone who had been really sick, and she said that the woman was on death's doorknob."

B.S. of Inver Grove Heights: "My wife just got our 2-year-old son out of his crib from his nap and went to change his diaper—and found that he was dry. We're trying to teach him to go to the bathroom on the toilet now. She said: 'You're as dry as a doornail.' "

Waiting for Luke Perry of Oakdale: "Today in class, I was trying to shout something across the room to someone, but she didn't hear me. So I looked at my faithful friend Sarah and said: 'Gosh, Michelle is deaf as a doorknob.' "

M.M.M. of Woodbury: "My daughter is going active Army, and last night, she told her dad that she was going to be traveling to Colorado. He says: 'That'll be nice for you. Maybe it would be more comfortable if you traveled in your skivvies.' "

Midlife Mom of New Richmond, Wis.: "My favorite malapropism is a matter of public record. Minnesota senator Magnus Johnson thought Congress was moving much too slow on an agricultural bill. He asked his fellow senators to take the bull by the tail and look him straight in the eye."

Speckity of Lake Elmo: "One day, a dear friend of mine was inviting us over for lunch. She said that she had some great sandwich makings: turkey and bread and great beefcake tomatoes."

Vern of St. Paul: "My ex-wife once—in the process of changing her mind over some little decision, when I challenged her on it—said: 'Well, it's a woman's Purgatory to change her mind.' "

BULLETIN BOARD REPLIES: We will resist all obvious retorts.

Grammie Deb of River Falls, Wis.: "My friend's mom was a major Ms. Malaprop. Two of my favorites:

"1) 'We'll burn that bridge when we get to it.'

"2) During the Persian Gulf War, she was very upset because her friend's nephew was being shipped overboard."

Casey of St. Paul: "In a staff meeting, a co-worker said something was not worth the ink it was written on."

K.F. of St. Paul: "I was making cookies with my friend S.P. Angela the other day, and she said to me: 'Well, we'd better make these soon. That oven is hotter than a Banshee.' "

Lucy of St. Paul: "My dad said the funniest thing today. We're in the car, and he's talking about how I don't know anything about life 'cause I'm only 17, and he says: 'You're only a sand in the grain of time.' "

Judy of Bayport: "My friend Margie in Monterey, California, has two sons, a full-time job and three part-time jobs. I was talking to her right before Christmas, and she was feeling quite harried with all of the Christmas preparations. She told me: 'I'm knee-deep in my elbows.' "

LeAnna of Cottage Grove: "A girlfriend of mine at work, when the weather is little bit chilly, says: 'It's nipply outside.' "

BMW of the Midway: "My mother, who was a nursing student in the early '60s, had a Norwegian friend who was very concerned with her skin. After a small breakout of pimples, she was heard to exclaim, 'Look at all the nipples on my face!' "

Leah of Minneapolis: "I used to work with a guy who always said 'nip it in the butt.' I never had the heart to correct him, because it always cheered my day up to have him say 'nip it in the butt.' "

Homeless of Woodbury: "It looked like it was about to clear up on one of those rainy days we've been having lately, and my husband thought he saw a rainbow. But he said: 'Nope. It was just a pigment of my imagination.' "

Anonymous woman: "My friend and I were discussing why he did not like to date younger women. He said it's because they're still a little green behind the ears."

Theresa of the East Side: "My boyfriend and I went on a cruise in March, and this lady was talking about something that had sounded really funny to her. She said it brought tears to her ears."

Red of Hastings: "I had a lady in my store today, and she says: 'I think that guy has too many arms in the fire.' "

Wayne of Chisago City: "We're getting ready to finish our new house, and the other day my wife said: 'We don't have time to do everything. I just have too many fires in the furnace.' "

Sherb of Exeland, Wis.: "I was talking to a co-worker at the bank about a mutual friend of ours. My co-worker says: 'Oh, she's got too many fires in the pot already.'

"Now, this co-worker isn't much for cooking, so maybe she *does* know what she's talking about."

B.C. of St. Paul: "My brother was talking about how his jeans were too small, and he said: 'My love seats hang over the side.' "

Barbara of St. Paul and **Chris** of St. Louis Park: "We work with a lot of clients and attend a lot of meetings, and we collect these malapropisms. The top two are from our general collection. The others are all from a former staff person here who had a genius for being about 5 degrees off. She is gone, alas, and we honor her memory by sending these to you.

" 'The jury is still out to lunch.'

" 'I hope this isn't too much of a hairball idea.'

" 'I read that book from front to cover.'

" 'I'm afraid I was kind of a wet sponge.'

" 'Don't mind me; I'm just talking out loud here.'

" 'There's no three ways about it.' "

Duncan of Golden Valley: "Someone was talking to a friend of mine, telling about a first date she'd been on, and how she was really appalled when she was prepositioned the first time out."

Randy of Osceola, Wis.: "My brother Rod, from Tucson, asked me my capability of doing something, and I said: 'Well, it's like riding a bicycle. Once you forget, you never know how.' "

Dave of St. Paul: "A friend announced one day at work that she had to go to the optician because she needed a 'len' for her glasses."

Douglas of St. Paul: "A friend of mine told us that she had to go to the choirpractor. And then she was telling us how her back had got twisted around, and she said that it 'got screwed around her scrotum.' "

Crazy Brian of Lexington: "I work for a delivery service, and one that broke me to tears was one of the drivers saying to one of our dispatchers: 'I can read you like a glove.' "

Anonymous woman of St. Paul: "My ex-husband once told me—'course I can't believe everything he said—that when he was in Sunday school, he grew up thinking that one of the commandments was 'Thou shalt not commit a dog trick.' "

BULLETIN BOARD NOTES: We hate to engage in idle speculation, but maybe he never stopped thinking that. Who can guess how many failed marriages can be attributed to such simple misunderstandings?

Dick of Cottage Grove: "We're sittin' talkin' to a guy who just got a job tonight, and my wife was thinking he's quite intelligent. This was a maintenance job, and she told him it would be a piece of gravy."

Claire of St. Paul: "I was at a meeting the other day, and some guy said that something that he had experienced was just like the gravy on the cake."

Scott of St. Paul: "When I was a kid, we were visiting my grandparents with my parents, and my mother—trying to praise her mother-in-law's cooking—decided to ask, as we sat down to a sumptuous fried-chicken meal, whether the gravy we were having on the mashed potatoes was 'real chicken droppings gravy.' I think she meant to say 'drippings.' "

Sergeant Bilko of St. Paul: "A dear young thing in our office is working on a grant proposal. She averred that she needed to flush it out."

Nancy of St. Paul: "I was working at a local nursing home, which shall remain nameless. I was touring a prospective resident's family. *[BULLETIN BOARD INTERJECTS: Interesting image.]* One inquisitive family member asked, 'Do you separate the alert residents from the decapitated ones?' It was all I could do to keep from getting hysterical and wetting my pants."

Lynn of Falcon Heights: "We have a friend who tells us about the Cistern Chapel in Rome."

Liz of Stillwater: "My dear sister-in-law, whom I love with all my heart, is notorious for destroying the English language. One day I heard her accuse my brother of grinning like Chester the cat. And on another occasion, we were at the zoo and were talking about whether we wanted to get a drink, and she said: 'Yes, I could wet my weasel.' "

Lenette of Stillwater: "Years ago, my parents and I went out for an evening at the Chanhassen Dinner Theatre. Just before dinner, the waitress asked us if we cared for a cocktail from the bar.

"My father said, yes, we would: 'We'd like a carcass of wine.'

"The waitress smiled politely and left the table. She was probably going off to rest in the lounge and laugh herself silly."

Owen of Inver Grove Heights: "One day at work, one of our young female co-workers was telling of her college days, and she said that when she was a freshman in college, she and her friends would drink themselves into Bolivia every weekend."

Anonymous woman: "We once knew a bartender here—I'm in a small town in southeast Minnesota—who forever had us spitting beer out of our noses, because she would say things like: She had a friend who was so sick they had to put him in insulation, and another friend who had a baby that was so small they had to put it in the incinerator."

Les Funn of Minneapolis: "The other day, a co-worker got *very* upset—and was describing how she felt to the person she was upset with. She said: 'I am just vivid with you.' She continued by asking: 'I want to know what in carnation is going on here.' "

Leo of St. Paul: "My sister-in-law was out shopping at Bachman's to buy some flowers. She was walking around looking at the flowers—and asked the clerk: 'What are these purple and red and pink flowers up here?' And the guy said: 'Those are hanging clematis.' And she said: 'Oh, OK. Well, I'm gonna walk around and look at a few other things.'

"So she looked at some other flowers and came back, and she points up and says to the guy: 'I think I'll take that purple hanging clitoris.' "

Jeff R. of St. Paul: "I was talking to my sister about Christmas last year, and I said: 'So what did you get for Christmas?'

"She said she had gotten some clothes, and some money, and a placenta plant, and some perfume.

"I said: 'Wait a minute. You got a placenta plant?'

"She said: 'Yeah.'

"I said: 'What kind of plant?'

"She said: 'A placenta plant—you know, the ones with the big red flowers.'

"I said: 'You mean a poinsettia plant?'

"She said: 'Oh. Yeah. Whatever.' "

Becky of the East Side: "I have a girlfriend who uses the wrong word whenever she's trying to explain something to me that requires a word over two syllables. She called me up one day and described a gentleman she'd met in a bar in Stillwater. It goes like this: 'He was an older man, from Germany, who owns a restaurant where they serve Barbarian-type food.' "

T. of St. Cloud: "I was talking to a friend of mine about a lecture we had attended, and the lecture was . . . well, it wasn't the greatest, but my friend thought it was a little too poetic, a little too urethral."

Bill of Bethel College: "My dad had an electrical wholesale business in Des Moines. I was working at the counter one time, and a gentleman walked in and asked for an ovulating fan that would be suitable for hanging on the wall."

Kathy of Maplewood: "I'm calling to tell you about a girl I work with. I'll call her Rosebud. She's a hair stylist. She colored one of her clients' hair last week, and when her client got all done, she asked if there was any special care she should take—if she should be careful about swimming, getting water on it. Rosebud said: 'No, no, go ahead. You can swim. But be careful,' she said, 'because at this time of year, the urination level is so high in the water.' "

Grandma Joyce of Inver Grove Heights: "A friend was telling us about someone who had died and been cremated—and they put his ashes in a urinal."

BULLETIN BOARD MUSES: *This is what is known as adding insult to injury.*

Grandma Joyce, again: "My friend has done it again. Today, she was telling us about a fellow who was struck by lightning, and my friend's brother-in-law happened to see it happen, and he ran out and gave this fellow artificial insemination—but he didn't make it."

Kitty of St. Paul: "I was at my friend's house, and someone asked me a question. I didn't know the answer, so I just sorta stood there. And my friend said: 'Cat got your tail?' "

David of Roseville: "My brother gave me some advice several years back. He said: Women are like streetcars. The ocean is full of them."

Berly of Albert Lea: "I was lamenting the impending end of a relationship a couple of weeks ago, and my brother looked at me very seriously and said: 'That's OK. There's other chickens in the sea.' "

J.C. of parts hereabouts: "I was over at a friend's house the other day. He happens to be building his own place, and he was showing me around. He started commenting on how much work he had to do, and he said: 'You know, sometimes I feel like I run around here like a chicken with my legs cut off.' "

J.D. of St. Paul: "I have a Mrs. Malaprop that is one of my very own—I'm proud to say. I was scurrying around at work one day, and I said: 'Geez, I'm running around with my chicken cut off!' "

Sergeant Sue of Apple Valley: "Yesterday, in a meeting, a woman was trying to read some notes she had written out earlier and commented: 'I just can't seem to read my own hen peckings here.' "

M.B. of Roseville: "I work with a dear lady named Rosie. One day, she was getting impatient with someone and said: 'I wish they would s— or cut bait.' "

Jones of Rochester: "My wife and her sister are pregnant, and are due about the same time. We were talking, early on, about how her sister was having a rough time with morning sickness. My wife said that when they were growing up, her sister tended to throw up every once in a while.

"She said: 'Well, it's nothing new. She could puke on a dime.' "

Becca of Mahtomedi: "I caught myself doing one. I said: 'Yeah, these days I cry at the drop of a dime.' It sounded a lot like something my mom might say."

Jane of Bloomington: "I've been having lots of workers in my house, fixing the plumbing and working on our basement. One of the men was talking to me, and he said: 'You know, I know that song like the back of my head.' "

Jesse of North Branch: "My best friend is really a great person, but can get a tad mixed-up sometimes. We were driving through town when I questioned her turn at an intersection. She said: 'Oh, come on! I know these roads like the back of my neck!' "

Linda of St. Paul: "My cousin's boss frequently says: 'Well, that's no skin out of my nose.' It's painful to think about it."

Red of Oakdale: "I was sitting with some friends today—these are all men, by the way—listening to them discuss the soon-to-be-ex-wife of one of them. The discussion was getting pretty heated, and suddenly one guy said: 'She's lying through her nose.' "

Lee of White Bear Lake: "My husband told me once that you can't kick a gift horse in the teeth."

Mark of Shoreview: "I was in Cape Cod and went to a newsstand to get a local map. They gave me one, and I asked how much it was, and they said it was free. I was surprised. The woman said: 'Take it. Don't bite a gift horse in the mouth.' "

Morning Glory of Arden Hills: "I can tell you that Mrs. Malaprop is alive and well and living in Arden Hills. I think it must be me, because for *years* I have said: 'Never look a gift horse in the eye.' "

Kim of way up north: "I have a very dear but flighty sister-in-law who was telling me that somebody had said something to her that made her mad—and she said: 'Kim, I just had to grin and bite my teeth.' "

Karen of Roseville: "While returning to Minneapolis on the plane, as lunch was being served, I heard from somewhere back of me: 'Never bite the mouth that feeds you.' "

Jimbo of St. Paul: "A friend was tellin' me about havin' a beer in class in the morning and gettin' caught. She said she brought it because she needed to bite the hair of the dog."

Jean of Hastings: "Recently we were in Colorado, skiing. On the second day, we were making our way across an icy parking lot and witnessed an elderly man slip and almost wipe out. We overheard him say to his companion: 'I nearly bit the farm that time.' "

Christi of Woodbury: "My brother Rit is the king of the malaprops. I thought I'd heard 'em all, but yesterday's was the best.

"We were in his car, on some errands, and he was talking about something someone had said to him that was kinda rude, and he said: 'I don't know. I think that was just their way of breaking the wind.'

"I said: 'What?'

"And he said: 'I think that was just their way of breaking the wind—you know, like trying to get acquainted.'

"I said: 'You mean "breaking the ice"?'

"And he said: 'Oh, yeah. I guess that would be something else, huh?' And then he goes: 'What does that mean, anyway?'—and I had to tell him; this is a 26-year-old.

"So he's kind of a goober, but he's my big brother, and we all love him."

Anonymous man: "I was sitting in a meeting today, and a couple of guys there were talking; they couldn't decide what they wanted to do. They had different ideas about things, and one guy finally says: 'Well, we gotta make a decision here. We can't be flatulating back and forth.' "

J.D. of St. Paul: "A girlfriend of mine and I were at work, discussing the Xerox man and how unsociable he was. And my friend said: 'I don't think the Xerox people are supposed to flatulate with us.' "

B.J. of Maplewood: "I was sitting in the break room with a co-worker while she told me about all of the money she spent on a recent shopping trip. She ended her story with: 'I spent so much money that my husband had a hemorrhoid.' "

Sue of Little Canada: "My husband was just talking about how he had a chance to go to Brazil—a while back, before we were married. He said the reason he really wanted to go is because he wanted to soil his oats."

J.D. of Oakdale: "At a public meeting last night, a question regarding a difficult task to be done was directed to the group leader. He answered: 'We will get this done by nook or by cranny.' "

Anonymous woman: "A girlfriend and I were just driving to Rainbow, and I kept asking her a question over and over and over again, and she looked at me and said: 'Well, you're going to have to excuse me. I'm as deaf as a bat.' "

Buffy of Lake Elmo: "My 15-year-old son was telling me about someone he knows with Alzheimer's disease. Then he mentioned this other elderly woman he knows, and he said: 'I don't think *she* has it, because she's still as sharp as a bat.' "

Petey of St. Paul: "My husband is Mr. Malaprop. He tries really hard to get it right, but . . . the other night, he was saying that he really understood what was going on, and he said: 'You know, I'm smart as a tack.' "

The Eccentric Reprobate of White Bear Lake: "My German mother-in-law, Frau Malaprop, is visiting for the holidays. We get along great because she and my wife are 'two peaches in a pod.' "

Susan of Bayfield, Wis. "I once wrote an essay in college, and it read: 'The woman fell and lay prostitute on the ground.'

"The professor's note of correction read: 'The word you want is "prostrate." There is a difference between a fallen woman and one who has temporarily slipped.' "

CHAPTER 4

Our Pets, Ourselves

What would we do without 'em?

Chow, baby! *A collection of oddball pet gourmets—and WARNING! THREATS TO CONTENTED DINING LURKING HEREIN:*
Big Man, Big Man of White Bear Lake (who sounded more than a bit like Bill Murray in *Caddyshack*):

"Well, to tell the truth, I don't believe I'm calling—but, oh well.

"Basically, I've seen in your little section of the paper, during the last year or so, something called 'Cuisine Comique' (whatever; food blowing up in your kitchen), 'You Are What You Eat' (people eating incredibly strange things)—and for some reason, today, it popped into my head that you never had something like 'Your Pets Are What They Eat,' or whatever. I think that could be a really, really cool thing—like, you know, strange things that people feed to their pets.

"Like, one of my pets enjoys cough drops. In fact, he's looking at me very strange now that I've said it, and I'll have to give him one.

"It's really weird—and before anyone starts calling in, like, 'Oh, my God, listen to him! He gives his pets cough drops! They're gonna die!': My vet told me that Sammy, my little dog, could.

"So, oh well, it could be cool."
Tristan of the East Side: "I have a black Lab. He's about 3 years old; his name is Homer. During that three years, he's eaten, oh, my kitchen floor, a $1,500 antique teddy bear, endless shoes. Plus, he'll eat pocket lint if I hand it to him."
Mom of Roseville: "When my first son was an infant and he'd just started eating the sloppy cereal stuff, I had him in his infant seat on the floor in the family room. When I was done feeding him, he had this sloppy stuff all over his face.

"I thought it was pretty cute, because it was my first child, and I went to get the camera. When I came back, his face was clean—and I couldn't figure out how he did it. Then, I realized that he had been licked clean by our 90-pound black Lab."

Betty of Barnum: "A 'dog friend' of mine in England told me in a recent letter that a pointer she had years ago ate a 10-foot scarf!!!!!

"She said she saw him hunkered down as if he was trying to pass grass. She saw a bit of something protruding from his 'oompie,' put a plastic bag on her hand, grasped the object and out it came—hand over hand, a 10-foot-long scarf!

"The dog suffered no ill effects from this unusual meal. Top *that* one."

Melissa of White Bear Lake: "My dog once ate an entire sofa. She's also eaten a remote control, high-heeled shoes, a pair of glasses, carpet. The list just goes on."

Alice & Sam of Roseville: "We have a black Lab (named Babe) with a voracious, nondiscriminating appetite.

"She's eaten all the ordinary things: shoes, bars of soap, orthodontic retainers, an antibiotic prescription—pills, bottle and all.

"When she was a pup, she ate a picket fence that ringed our back porch. Each day, when we came home, we would discover one or two pickets missing and several nails that she had spit out!

"Another time, we locked her in the kitchen when we went to work. Wise to her ways, we sprayed all the wooden chairs and table legs with a dog repellent that our vet had 'guaranteed' would do the trick. I forgot something—and came back to find her licking off the repellent. I sprayed more. When we returned, one chair was missing all the legs, and the table was balancing on three legs.

"In spite of all she has eaten, she never has gotten sick—except once. That time, on Christmas Eve, she accidentally was shut in our garage with a half-gallon of cooking oil left over from a fondue, which had been put there to cool. When we discovered her, she looked decidedly bilious. She weaved into the living room and promptly threw up all over the gifts under the Christmas tree!"

Pam of Apple Valley: "Our neighbors' dog ate a Brillo pad! Ate the whole Brillo pad! For a long time, it wobbled around like it was dead drunk. And then it recovered and was fine."

Barbie Doll of River Falls, Wis.: "I have a dog that loves to eat crayons—and since I have a 3-year-old who likes to leave crayons around, the dog gets all he wants. As a side benefit of this—almost a simple pleasure, you might say—I get to clean up technicolor dog poop the next day."

Julie of Hudson, Wis.: "My dog Tippy, when she was a puppy, used to go out in the yard and eat rocks. She'd swallow 'em. I mean big, huge ones. She'd come inside, and she'd look guilty, like she'd done something really wrong, and then all of a sudden, she'd go off into the kitchen, on the linoleum floor, and you'd hear this awful sound. It was like: 'Retch, retch, retch, clunk. Retch, retch, clunk.' "

Amy of Mendota Heights: "If our dog Barney sees a can of whipped cream, his ears perk up. We hold the can way above his head, and he laps up the stream as it comes out."

Stephanie of Oakdale: "I want to tell you about my fiancé's parents' dog. His name is Rocky. He's a springer spaniel, and he eats everything. His favorite thing to do is: They have a garden in the backyard, and when he doesn't think anybody's looking, he . . . real . . . slowly . . . walks to the garden, looks around, reaches in, rips a cucumber off the vine, runs, hides and eats it. He thinks nobody sees him, and he does this every year."

Jennifer of Little Canada: "When I was a teenager, growing up on the farm, I had a horse named Jessica Jones. She loved to chew bubble gum. The cool thing is: She never swallowed it; she'd always spit it out after she'd chewed it for a while."

Shirley of Marine on St. Croix: "I've got a story about what pets won't eat. We had a Chihuahua that weighed a pound and a half when we got her. Paid $30 a pound. One time when she was off her feed, the vet said to give her junior baby food. You know how small that's chopped. But when she was finished, there was a ring of carrots that she'd just pushed out all around the dish. She refused to eat them."

BULLETIN BOARD MUSES: Forever putting the lie to the pernicious myth that Chihuahuas are stupid.

Becca of Mahtomedi: "My dogs' favorite food in the whole world is moldy hamburger buns. They will do *anything* for 'em—and let me tell you: Around here, we have a lot of those. Whatever you want them to do, they'll do it for moldy hamburger buns.

"And my cat eats earwax. She *loves* earwax. She'll just purr. The way I found this out is so gross: I was cleaning my ears out with a Q-Tip, and I threw the Q-Tip in the garbage, and I came back into the bathroom a little while later, and she had tipped the garbage over and dug through and found an earwax-filled Q-Tip and was eating it. It was so gross."

Rocky of God's Country North: "My grandmother had a huge watchdog named Bronco. One day, we watched out the kitchen window as Bronco chased around and around. We thought he had his tail, but no, it was something else.

31

"Grandma puts a baggie over her hand, goes out and extracts a pair of pantyhose. Being the good recycler she is, she said she thought she could just wash 'em up like new.

"Brrrr. Makes you think."

Postpartum Mom of Woodbury: "Following the birth of my son, his dad and I anxiously awaited the day his umbilical-cord stump would fall out so we could inspect it, even though it reeked. As the cord was hanging by a thread, we knew the next diaper change would allow us to check out the decaying stump.

"The suspense mounted as we eagerly undressed the baby—but we were shocked to see the stump missing, and nowhere to be found. We were shaking out his clothes and diaper when we heard a crunching sound from the direction of our pet Sheltie, Kirby.

"You guessed it. Kirby ate that rank stump. In my postpartum blues, I bawled about his lack of respect for the last physical link between mother and child."

Ughamania of Balsam Lake, Wis.: "Stubby was a small mixed-breed dog—short legs; that's why he got the unimaginative name of Stubby. Stubby lived with us for 16 years, and he would eat *anything*—anything except Jell-O.

"But I didn't call to tell you about what Stubby wouldn't eat; I wanted to tell you about his preference for Pepsi regular. We gave him Pepsi one time in a saucer, and he loved it. Later, we switched to a diet cola of another brand, and he would not drink it.

"We thought that odd, so we tested him with clear sodas and other brands of colas—but he never touched 'em. We even went so far as to try pouring other colas into a regular Pepsi can and pouring it in the saucer; he knew the difference. We even took Diet Pepsi and put it in the regular Pepsi can, and he still would not drink it. We could not fool him. We tried every possible combination, and he would not drink 'em.

"Stubby has been gone from us for two years now. Bless his little heart. We hope that wherever he's at, he's still getting a slug of regular Pepsi."

Nancy of Lakeville: "My maternal grandmother had a mutt named Blue. She was very fat. One day, we went over to visit, and the dog was sitting in the kitchen in front of a kitchen chair; on the chair was a paper plate with a piece of toast, butter on it. So my mom's talking to Grandma, and this dog's howlin' and howlin'.

"My mom's like: 'Shut up, Blue. Shut up!' Finally she says: 'What is wrong, Ma? What's wrong with this dog?' Grandma very seriously turned to her and said: 'Oh, we're out of jelly.'

"Couldn't believe it; what a spoiled dog."

Shut that door! From **Dick** of Woodbury:

"Last December, I called in about our new dog, Sam, who I thought was pretty smart because she went under the Christmas tree, tore open a package of nuts, and then, without help from any human, was somehow able to take the cover off the jar.

"Well, I want you to know: That dog is not smart at all. She has taught herself how to open the sliding doors that go out to our patio and how to open the sliding screen doors to go out to the patio once the main doors are open—but no matter how I try, I can't teach that dumb dog how to *close* the doors."

Stupid Pet Predicaments:

Dahlia of Lexington: "Here it is, 5:30 in the morning, and I woke up to the sound of paper rustling. I have three cats, and one of them, Pookie—if there's any mischief to get into, she will find it. I had left an almost-empty bag of potato chips on the counter last night, planning to throw them out for the birds this morning. Pookie evidently wanted a snack sometime during the night, so she jumped up on the counter and stuck her head in the bag.

"I followed the rustling sound, and here's Pookie: She had fallen off the counter and was stuck in the little space between the counter and the stove, meowing this embarrassed little meow, with the potato-chip bag completely over her head.

"My other two cats were standing there all frantic, like: Can you believe that cat?

"Pookie is fine now, but she keeps licking her lips from the salt, and the fur on her head is a little greasy."

Jim Boelter of West St. Paul: "When my yellow Lab was a young puppy, he liked to chew anything and everything. Well, one day I came home from work and I heard some whimpering. I went into the dining room, and his nose was tight up against the wall.

"I bent down and saw that he had a strand of carpet in his mouth. Backed him off a little bit; probably pulled about 12 feet of carpet out of his throat and stomach. Evidently, what he had done was: He started chewing at one end of the room, kept chewing, and got stuck at the far end of the room.

"Rather strange."

Jeff of Eau Claire, Wis.: "It was kind of a coincidence when I saw Jim's pet predicament in the paper. The same day, I noticed where my Lab threw up chunks of carpet. I figured: Well, she's learned her chewing lesson.

"But later on, when I'm out taking her for a walk, she dumps, and there's about a four-foot-long carpet thread hanging out; it was apparently longer, hung up somewhere inside. All I could think of was the mounting vet bills.

"Well, later on that day, she voided it; I know 'cause I hit it with the lawn mower, and carpet shot everywhere. It was quite a ball of thread.

"Kinda gives new meaning to the term 'carpet pile.' Talk about your high-fiber diet!

"Apparently, a lot of dogs like eating carpet. Maybe someone should invent a new dog food. Call it Carpet-O's."

J.W. of Chisago County: "You know how the Easter grass gets all over, from the kids' Easter baskets? Well, my cat always seems to get ahold of at least one piece— and the reason I always know he has is because he has a little piece of Easter grass sticking out of his butt. It is hard on both of us to pull that little thing out."

Precious, go home! Wrote **JB's Wife:**

"About two years ago, we adopted a dog from the local animal shelter, and since the family couldn't agree on a name for her, we decided to stick with the name she came with: Precious!!! I really feel stupid going outside and yelling 'Here, Precious!' and this full-grown black Lab comes bounding across the yard. Luckily for us, we live on a farm, so there are no neighbors nearby to hear us.

"I had convinced the rest of the family, except JB, to name the dog Grandma. I thought it would be fun to tell the kids, 'Did you remember to feed Grandma this morning?'; 'Grandma didn't mean to bite you'; or 'I sure hope Grandma doesn't run away!' Somehow, it just isn't the same with a dog named Precious.

"In the first year we had her, Precious chewed through the new plastic edging around the garden, the seat belt of our car, JB's glasses, and anything in the garage that wasn't nailed down. I'm sure Grandma would never have done anything like that."

Sarah of St. Paul: "I had a biology teacher in high school, almost 20 years now, and he had a dog named Ye—'cause then when he'd go out to call the dog, it'd be: 'Here, Ye! Here, Ye!' "

Rita of Lake Elmo: "My brother had a puppy once, and he named it Quat—so every time he'd call it, he'd say: 'Come, Quat!' "

Gayle the Paint Lady of Shoreview: "Years ago, when I had horses, my horseshoer had a dog named Fetch—so that when he called it, the dog didn't know if it was coming or going."

Cindie of Shoreview: "We have a Yorkie that we call Echo. To call her inside, we go: '**ECHO,** ECHO, echo. . . .' "

Timber Toes of St. Paul: "My friend just got a really cute border collie, and her dad got to name it. He named it Reagan. He did this because now he can say: 'Sit, Reagan! Heel, Reagan! Beg, Reagan!' *[BULLETIN BOARD MUSES: Wake up, Reagan!]* He *loves* it."

Jim of St. Paul: "We've got two dogs. One's named Albert, and the other's named Einstein. I get a real roar every time I hear my mate call out the back window in the summertime: 'Albert! Einstein! Get out of the garden.' The neighbors must think we're crazy."

Katie of Vadnais Heights: "My dog's name is Moo. She looks like a Holstein cow. And to the people who felt stupid yelling 'Elvis!' or 'Precious!' out their door: Try Moo-ing out the back door."

Kris of Como Park: "When we were growing up, we had a family cat named Hooker. We named it after Robert Redford in *The Sting*. Fancy calling after that cat in the neighborhood."

Lori H. of Spooner, Wis.: "I have to tell you about a pet name I holler out my back door. It's my neighbors' dog, and I've tried everything to get them to keep him quiet. Called the cops. Sweet-talked the owner. Called the city clerk about the animal-control ordinance. The owner was right: Hollering the dog's name shuts him up. But I'm a recovering alcoholic, and now I'm yelling 'Hooch.' "

Kathy of Eagan: "I have a dog named Guilty. She's a German shepherd. She's lots of fun, and she's got a great personality, but she's a bit destructive. So I thought Guilty would be the perfect name: Either she looks guilty, she is guilty, or she makes me feel guilty." *BULLETIN BOARD MUSES: Furthermore, it's a fabulous name—"Guilty!"—for those times when a little discipline is in order. And what could be more fun than barking "Guilty!" out the back door, in apparent judgment of all the world?*

Pat of St. Paul: "I have always wanted to have a dog. I don't, but if I did, I'd name her Stella. Every time I'd yell for it out the back door, I could hold the edge of my T-shirt—in agonizing fashion, just like Stanley in *A Streetcar Named Desire*—and yell out: 'Stell-aaaaaa.' "

Gladys of St. Cloud: "About 30 years ago, my older brothers, Jerry and Matt, named our farm dog Woof. They claimed it was the dog's first word." *BULLETIN BOARD OBSERVES: Easy enough to verify.*

Kathy of Cottage Grove: "My parents had a cleaning lady who lived on a farm, and her kids or her grandkids—I'm not sure which—found a cat. They called it Ben—and then Ben had kittens. They had to change the name to Ben Her."

Dorothy Terry of White Bear Lake: "We had a little beagle named Please. It was a good name for our kids, because it taught them a few manners: 'Get up, Please.' 'Sit down, Please.' "

Joanne of St. Paul: "At one time, I worked with a woman who was a registered dietitian. She had two dogs, and their names were Sam 'n' Ella."

Missy of West St. Paul: "I have two very computer-literate friends who named their new kittens Bit and Byte. This also fits their temperaments. Later on, they acquired an Angora kitten that they called Microsoft."

Craig of South St. Paul: "Several years ago, my wife and I went to the local animal shelter and picked up a couple of male kittens. On the way home, we decided to name them Cliff and Norm.

"Problem was: We seem to have gotten it backwards. When anybody would be sitting around having a beer, the cat named Cliff would absolutely climb up your body to get at that beer. Just went crazy; there was no stopping him. And the one named Norm meowed incessantly."

Old One-eyed Dog Face: "When I used to live up in northern Minnesota, in the woods, the guy down the road from me took in a couple little kittens. He named 'em Scratch and Sniff. Pretty cute cat names.

"He'd only had 'em a couple weeks, and we were playin' with 'em out in the yard when a big old hawk come swoopin' right out of the sky, comes right down and grabs Scratch and carries him off, never to be seen again.

"So what happened was: Scratch got scratched, and then there was only Sniff. Sniff."

J.D. of Minneapolis: "I have a cautionary example of three kittens we named—outside kittens. Named 'em Hickory, Dickory and Doc. Dickory met his demise, unfortunately, and to call the cats in for dinner after that was pretty tough. I think Doc has gotten over it, but 'Hickory! . . . pause . . . Doc!' really didn't work.

"Caution. Be careful what you name 'em."

Gypsi of St. Paul: "When we first got our kitten, three years ago, he was really young and had no personality. He'd copy our older cats with every move they made, so we named him Xerox the Copy Cat. I thought that was cute." *BULLETIN BOARD NOTES: Yes, but it's our strong hunch that those eternally vigilant, notoriously fretful trademark attorneys at the Xerox Corporation will not find this little matter, as you put it, "cute." People start naming their furry little domestic animals after your trademarked products—and the next thing you know, you're out of business! But worry not, Gypsi; we will protect your identity at any and all costs.*

Shannon of Apple Valley: "When we got our kitten a few years ago, my husband and I were going back and forth, trying to decide what we should name it, and finally he said: 'Why don't we name it Makita?'

"I thought: 'That's cool'—and after he'd been named that for quite some time, I come to find out that's a power-drill brand name! *[BULLETIN BOARD NOTES: actually, a whole line of home-shop equipment.]* I felt really stupid, naming our pet after a power drill.

"So when people ask 'Oh, what does that mean?' I say: 'That means "my kitty" in Japanese.' People always say: 'Oh, really?' "

Spock of Minneapolis: "My wife fosters for the Animal Relief Fund—and although I don't care to have all the little kittens in my house, I do get the job of naming them. We've had six of them named after blender speeds: Whip, Puree, Blend, Chop, Dice and Liquefy. We've had dictators: Lenin, Stalin, Hitler; we had to throw in a Himmler, although he didn't make it. And right now, we have five Marx brothers in there: Groucho, Chico, Harpo, Zeppo and Gummo. Groucho actually does have a mustache, like Groucho Marx.

"I just wish that the people who adopt these kittens after we foster them were forced to use the names that I gave them."

Jenny of Mankato: "My husband told me I could get a cat—on one condition: He got to name it. Well, he named our cat Alpo. You'd be amazed at how many idiots say: 'But isn't that a dog food?' "

BULLETIN BOARD MUSES: Idiots? Why are they idiots?

Julie of the West Side: "I acquired a pretty little red kitty cat from a friend of mine, and her name was Peaches. I figured that if I put a sign on my house that said 'This House Protected by Peaches,' nobody would pay any attention whatsoever—so I renamed her Pit Bull. Now the sign on my house says: 'Beware of Pit Bull.' "

Linda W. of Eagan: "My girlfriend had a Siamese cat, and she had her little nephew over and asked him if he wanted to help her name it. He was of . . . limited vocabulary. And he said: 'One.' And she said: 'We can't name a cat One. Think of another name.' And he said: 'Two.' So she named him Two."

Kate of Lindstrom: "A while back, my family and I got a big, fuzzy half–Great Pyrenees/half-collie puppy. The two kids and I agreed that Byron would be a great name for the dog—for reasons I won't go into. My husband, Dave, the lone holdout, was really opposed to the name and came up with ideas that the rest of us felt were really awful.

"After three weeks, the dog was still unnamed, and my husband still refused to let us call him Byron. When my husband came home from work one evening, I told him that I had thought of a great name—one that I knew he would like and appreciate, and one I was sure the dog would respond to. Then I called: 'Here, Dave! Come here, boy!' And the puppy came bounding into my arms.

"My husband agreed, then and there, to name the puppy Byron."

Vern of Roseville: "My son, who lives in Atlanta, had a common problem of Southern households: cockroaches. Not wanting to use poisons with a 2-year-old daughter, he opted for nature's solution, a cockroach-eating gecko lizard, whom he named Art. Art Gecko!"

Audrey of Shoreview Too: "I'm going to get myself a salamander, not that I've ever really wanted a salamander, just so that I can name it Newt Gingrich—who, may I add, I consider very aptly named."

Rachel of Stillwater: "Shortly after we named our dog Ginger, we found out just how popular her name was when friends came over with their dog, also named Ginger. We decided we had to modify her name, so we tried Ginge, Gingie—and finally settled on Gingivitis. Actually, Gingivitis has a nice ring to it if you don't associate it with dental gum disease." *BULLETIN BOARD NOTES: But we do associate it with gum disease. Can't help it. Don't know how we're gonna shake ourselves of that.*

August Rubrecht of the University of Wisconsin–Eau Claire: "This is for Rachel of Stillwater, who named her dog Gingivitis, as well as for other practitioners of canine onomastics. Be careful! Dogs live up to the standards set by their names.

"I have owned a long dynasty of bird dogs, always naming them strictly on phonetic principles. Meaning, I thought, was irrelevant. The name just had to be yellable and hard to confuse with the name of a hunting buddy or another dog.

"Looking back, though, I realize dogs with good ol' dog names—Lady, Clyde, Rhonda, Heidi *[BULLETIN BOARD MUSES: Rhonda?]*—were all pretty good ol' dogs. Hambone, with a food name, was a genius at finding birds but incredibly gluttonous. P.A. was just about totally worthless, a fact which doesn't seem to support my case until I reveal that P.A. stood for P— Ant.

"The principle was pointed out to me last season when I complained to a friend about my current dog's multiple deficiencies. She asked, 'What's his name?' 'Bozo.' 'Well, no *wonder!*'"

Judy of St. Paul: "We have a miniature wiener dog, and her name is Pee Wee. All the time."

Ray of St. Paul: "We once had a dog named Egypt. We called him that because he made pyramids all over the yard."

Tiffany Bose of Ladysmith, Wis.: "When we brought our new puppy home, we had trouble deciding on a name for him. When he went from room to room in our house, leaving piles as he went, a name for him became obvious; we started calling him 'Feckus.' Not too many people have figured out that 'Feckus' is really spelled F-E-C-E-S. The name stayed, and he's now a wonderful addition to our family."

BULLETIN BOARD REPLIES: A dog named Feces. We have now, officially, heard everything.

Mr. Lizard: Montessori teacher **Fiamma** of Forest Lake told us of a time when she had "critters living in my classroom and outside in a fenced-in yard: a boa constrictor named Doña Ibarra, several gerbils, lots of different-colored mice, Ping the Duck, a fire-bellied newt named Robin, numerous fish (no official names), Sir Thomas the Cat and Don Iguana.

"Now and then, Don Iguana would escape—like the time someone broke into the place and let everything out (except the fish). When Don Iguana got loose, I'd just grab him by his tail, he'd 'go stiff,' and I'd stick him back in his big cage. After living in my classroom many years, he and the cage had grown to be pretty big: The cage was six feet tall, and he was three feet long. The kids loved to feed him; we even made a cookbook called 'How to Feed an Iguana,' with the warning that iguanas do not like bananas.

"One nice sunny day, while the kiddos are outside playing under the pine trees, big ole Don Iguana decides to get out . . . again. Again I grab him by his tail, but instead of 'going stiff,' he begins twirling around and around and around so fast that I'm just panicked. And yes, of course, just as Mother Nature has designed, his body detaches, and I'm left with this writhing tail.

"Just then it's time for the kids to come back in (of course), so I yell to get the kids out. I, of course, should have just let them come in and see some of nature's protective measures! Ha! I felt like I was holding a baby's leg; I was one freaked-out teacher.

"Somehow we got Don Iguana back into his cage; the tail had stopped writhing, the kids were back inside, I'd put the tail on a tray (like any good Montessori teacher), and we were sitting around looking at poor Don Iguana when the tail started twitching AGAIN.

"I'd had it with Mother Nature, so I grabbed a shovel and the tail and went outside, dug a hole, dropped in the tail, covered it and gave the soil a good banging . . . just to be sure it wouldn't be jumping around anymore.

"When I got back inside, the kids wanted to know if another iguana would grow."

Laughing through the tears: From **Dick** of Mendota Heights:
"A few months ago, our blond Persian cat of 18-plus years developed kidney disease. We fed him special food, combed his beautiful hair, and watched as his weight diminished. We all knew that the end was near, but our kindly vet assured us that he was not suffering—and would eventually slip off into unconsciousness.

"Last Sunday afternoon, he did just that. After a few tears, we placed him in a box with his favorite blanket and set it outside near the door—the intention being to have our vet store the box until spring, when he could be buried with our other pets at the Feist Pet Cemetery.

"The following day, a married son stopped by unexpectedly, saw this box outside, and thought it was a delivery. He brought it inside—and, curious, opened it. What a surprise to see dead Richard.

"Shortly thereafter, when my wife heard about it, she started to say: 'Curiosity killed the . . .'—and she stopped."

Ah, the smell of puppy feet: From **D.G.** of Oakdale:

"Last evening while sitting in bed watching television, I noticed my wife smelling our Bichon's feet. I asked her what she was doing.

"Linda said she was having a simple pleasure: puppy feet.

"I asked: 'Smelling puppy feet is a simple pleasure?'

"She said they smell like popcorn.

"I tried—and sure enough, they smelled like popcorn. A bit stale, but popcorn nonetheless.

"Go figure."

BULLETIN BOARD NOTES: Daily B. Boarders will recall that in the wake of this little report from D.G. of Oakdale, readers all over got down on their hands and knees to sniff the feet of their puppies and their big old dogs and their cats and . . . well, God knows what else.

The Bulletin Board Hot Line took dozens of calls from newly enlightened companion humans and from longtime connoisseurs of aromatic canine extremities, who reported that their dogs' feet did, in fact, smell like popcorn, or Doritos, or Fritos . . . or dog.

Go figure.

One theory: urine. (Shudder.) A better one, we think, supplied by **Jane** *of West St. Paul:* "Dogs perspire through the pads of their feet. The salt in the perspiration combined with the skin oils gives off the same oily/salty smell we identify with the snack foods."

Said **Joanie B.** of St. Paul—who sounded eerily like Lloyd Bentsen talking to Dan Quayle: "The stale-popcorn smell is *not* from urine. I work as a lab tech, and I smell urine all . . . day . . . long. I know what urine smells like: fresh urine, old urine. It does not smell like popcorn."

Chris of Newport: "We've had two dogs with popcorn peds. In fact, when my son was younger, he once made this comment when we walked past a movie theater: 'That smells like Malcolm's feet.' "

Doodledog of St. Paul: "I was talking to my friend Mimi on the phone, and she says to me that she *loves* smelling her puppies' feet; she's got two dogs. She said she can tell one dog from the other just by smelling their feet. She says one is buttered, and the other is unbuttered."

Karl of St. Cloud: "I'm reading about all of these people sniffing their dogs' feet—and I'm thinking to myself: Wouldn't it be easier just to actually *make* some popcorn and then smell *that?* Besides, then you could eat it afterward—or is that being too logical?"

V.J. of St. Paul: "Maybe to put a cap on the whole situation, you could try taking some popcorn and soaking it in milk overnight. Then you let it sit somewhere for about a week—and you'll find out that it smells like a dog."

A.M. of Oakdale—being funny, we trust: "I was just calling to say that my hamster's feet smell like popcorn."

Pancho of Maplewood: "I don't know about dogs' feet and popcorn, but my ex-wife used to always tell me that when she was a kid, her dad's feet smelled like Cheetos. I never checked—and now I don't have to."

Butch of St. Paul, speaking for the crowd: "I can't believe it. I've got important things to *do*—and what do I do? I find myself . . . in . . . smelling . . . my dog's . . . feet! I can't *believe* it! All these things to do, and I'm in smelling the damn dog's feet!"

Anonymous woman: "I feel like the biggest idiot in the world.

"I have three dogs; that's 12 feet. I came home from a hard day at work, and I read Bulletin Board—all this *popcorn* stuff. So what have I been doing for the last 20 minutes? Crawling around on my kitchen floor, smelling 12 dog feet.

"I don't smell any popcorn.

"I think Bulletin Board has perpetrated a hysteria on the people of St. Paul, who are now *imagining* that they smell popcorn on their dogs' feet. What if I were to tell you that I smell my dogs' feet and smell toxic gas? Will our emergency rooms fill up?"

Mike of St. Paul: "After trying to smell my dog's feet, I *did* get a whiff of toxic gas . . . but I don't think it came from his feet."

F.J.E. of Maplewood—a rather older lady: "I am pretty sick of all of the stories about dogs' feet smelling like popcorn. Stick to the real stuff.

"I was just down to my cousin's farm, and I don't know what their German shepherd's feet smell like—but they have a calf, and his feet smelled just like pie. And I'm not saying what kind."

41

CHAPTER 5

You Great Big
Beautiful Dolls!

*T*errible *things can happen to dolls, and to the children who love them—but sometimes, when they're lucky, wonderful things follow:*

Patti of Woodbury: "My daughter Michelle has a doll—an American Girl doll named Samantha, whom she has loved so much that poor Sam's going bald because her hair's been brushed so much. Not to mention that she has no eyelashes.

"Her wonderful Grandma Mae, who gave her the doll two years ago and who loves dolls more than any child I know, asked my Michelle if she would like to have Samantha's hair replaced. Michelle said: Sure, that would be fine—so Grandma sent Samantha to the Pleasant Company Doll Hospital to get new hair.

"Well, lo and behold, when Sam came back—in her hospital gown and hospital bracelet—Pleasant Company had replaced her head, because it's cheaper to put a brand-new head on; they just don't replace hair.

"When Michelle opened up the box and saw that Sam had a new head, she said, 'Sam, you have a new head!'—and she was clearly disappointed.

"Grandma Mae felt so terrible that she called Pleasant Company about a week later and said: 'You know, I'm feeling really bad about what I did to my granddaughter's doll. Is there any chance you have the original head on file?' Pleasant Company said: 'Well, yes, as a matter of fact, we do have her original head.' And Grandma Mae said: 'Would you mind if I sent the doll back? Would you be willing to replace the new head with the original one, because my granddaughter just misses her real Sam so much.' And the Pleasant Company *very pleasantly* said: 'Well, we've never had a request like that, but we would be happy to do that.'

"So Sam is on her way back to Pleasant Company Hospital, where she'll get her original head back.

"I think that's just a really special story."

Lynn of Brooklyn Park: "When I was 10 years old, I used to go diving with my Barbie dolls—and as I was diving with Barbie, her head came off and went down the river in the current. I had to bury the Barbie doll body, because it was the Headless Barbie."

Pained of Lakeland: "My daughter Karen's dad shopped maniacally for a black My Size Barbie. Finally found her, and Karen said she would grow her hair longer to match Barbie's.

"Today, I woke up to a wastebasket full of lush hair. Karen said: 'It's quicker for Barbie to look like me.' "

Phil Conrad of WISM-FM radio in Eau Claire, Wis.: "Have a traumatic toy story for you. Happened about eight years ago, when my eldest daughter was 4 or 5.

"She was having an absolutely terrible day, and the one thing that gave her solace was a doll that we called Big Dolly, which was a huge rag doll with a plastic head and neck and yarn hair. A cute thing.

"At any rate, Rachel is having an absolutely terrible day: She's pitching fits; she's upset about this, she's upset about that, she's upset about the other thing. What she does when she's upset is to go and get Big Dolly and go off and sit in a chair and hug Big Dolly and rock Big Dolly, which is almost as big as she is.

"She is getting more and more wound up and more and more obnoxious in the course of the day. Finally, right before dinner would normally be, and dinner is not ready, she pitches a fit because dinner is not ready. Decides that she's going to stalk off with Big Dolly. Reaches down, grabs Big Dolly by the hair to pick Big Dolly up—and finds herself standing there with Big Dolly's severed head.

"You've never heard a scream like that in your life."

Mama Bear of White Bear Lake: "When I was little, in the mid-'50s, I had a hollow rubber doll named Squeaky. Squeaky was your typical rubber doll: She did not have hair; she had that molded sort of hair, the funny plastic eyes.

"One of our dogs tore one of Squeaky's arms off, and my mother tried absolutely everything she could to get that arm to stay back on. She tried tape; she tried melting it back on; nothing would work. So poor Squeaky has gone through life with only one arm. My parents tried to replace her with another doll, and nothing was quite the same as Squeaky.

"I still have Squeaky now, and she still has one arm. We used to have the arm that the dog chewed off; that's long since gone, but Squeaky still survives—one arm, and sad as heck."

The Tooth Fairy of Hastings: "My oldest daughter, Shiny Shannon, is now 24 and lives in Florida. When she was 3 years old, she had a favorite doll that had a vinyl head and a cuddly beanbag body that was covered with a bright pink material. It was just the right size for a 3-year-old to drag everywhere.

"She named the doll Pink Baby and loved it to tatters. Before Christmas, we mailed Pink Baby to Santa so the elves could repair her. Santa looked all over for another Pink Baby, but there weren't any. On Christmas morning, Pink Baby was under the tree, but her body was now fluorescent orange.

"It was always fun to watch well-meaning strangers try to convince this stubborn 3-year-old that her doll was orange. It was even more fun to see their reactions when the mom also called the doll Pink Baby."

An anonymous woman: "I don't have a story about doll rehabilitation, but I do have one about doll magic.

"When I was 4, we were extremely poor. I mean very, very poor. And even at 4, my hopes for what Christmas would bring were really slim. I remember it was winter, and my mother was in another room sewing something, and I was futzing around in her bedroom, and I opened her bottom dresser drawer—and there was the biggest, most beautiful baby doll I had ever seen.

"I yelled: 'Mommy! Mommy! There's a doll in your drawer!' I was astonished.

"To this day, I cannot remember how she distracted me, but by the time I got back into her bedroom to look in that drawer, the doll was gone. I was amazed; I *knew* I had seen it there.

"And my mother told me: 'Well, you know what happened. Fairies brought it, and you weren't supposed to see it, so they took it back until the time is right for you to have it.' And at 4, to me, even the disappointment of not getting that doll immediately was overridden by the magic of fairies coming into my house and leaving a doll.

"So time went on. It was probably not more than a couple of weeks—eternity, to a 4-year-old—and Christmas came, and sure enough, there under the tree was that beautiful baby. My sister had bought it for me, God bless her.

"And God bless the Salvation Army, who provided three other baby dolls. What a Christmas! What a Christmas for a poor kid.

"So we had the magic fairies, and we had the magic baby doll—and maybe it's not too early in the year to remind people that donations to things like Toys for Tots can make magic in some other kid's Christmas."

CHAPTER 6

Oh, And Were Their Faces Red!

A riot of embarrassing moments:

Arlene of St. Paul: "One Saturday night, my best friend and I got dressed up and headed out to a popular East Side bar. The place was packed, and I met this great-looking guy. We talked for a while, and then I excused myself and went to the ladies' room, fixed my hair and my makeup—trying to impress this guy.

"I walked back to the bar and was kinda flirting with him, when someone comes up from behind me and taps on my shoulder. I turned around, and this guy blurts out: 'Hey! I think someone's following you!'—and then started laughing hysterically and pointing at me. I turned 12 shades of red as I looked down to find a 25-foot trail of toilet paper stuck to the bottom of my boot."

Chris of St. Paul: "Many years ago, I was going out with a woman—had been dating her for about six months—when I took her to the wedding of an officemate of mine. As we were standing outside the reception area, about six of the most important people in my office, and their wives and dates, came up. So I started introducing everybody to her. I went through the line—said 'This is so-and-so, this is so-and-so, this is so-and-so.' And then I turned to her and said: 'Everybody, this is Renee.'

"I stopped for about five seconds, looked at her and said: 'That's not right, is it?' We broke up shortly after that."

Kurt of St. Paul: "I was eating in my car at the Hudson A&W drive-in. There was a cute girl in the next car over, and we sort of kept winking and smiling at each other during the meal.

"It was cold out, so I decided to close the window as far as I could with the food tray attached to it. As I'm closing it, I glance over at the girl, and she's glaring at me with this horrible expression on her face—like she's witnessing mass murder or something. I then noticed that the window wasn't going up too easily, and the reason was that my sheepdog's head was caught in it as he was trying to nibble at the tray from the back seat.

"I was so startled that I quick rolled down the window so far that the tray and glass mug and everything crashed to the ground. Needless to say, the cute girl wasn't overly impressed with me."

Plain Jane of the West Side: "This morning, I went to the farmers' market. I was wearing my salmon-colored T-shirt that those of us who volunteered for the Special Olympics wore. It was chilly, so I was also wearing a sweatshirt on top of it.

"As I'm roaming around amongst all the wonderful greenery down there, I see a man who's also wearing his T-shirt from the Special Olympics. I go to pull up my sweatshirt, to show him that I'm wearing mine—and lo and behold, I get hold of both the T-shirt and the sweatshirt, and I pull up, and I'm standing there showing the guy my boobs!

"He looks at me, stunned, and I go, 'Oops.' I had to get out of there."

Dale of Eau Claire, Wis.: "A friend was doing some last-minute Christmas shopping. She had her arms full of packages, and because it was sloppy weather, she needed a new pair of boots. She was seated in a trying-on chair, and the salesperson was helping. As she struggled to fit her foot into the boot, she unfortunately passed gas rather loudly. The salesman excused himself and mumbled something about having to find a slightly larger pair of boots for her.

"She was extremely embarrassed and shy, so she gathered the packages and headed out the door. Unfortunately, she discovered after she went to the car to drop her packages off that she had left behind one of the harder-to-find packages.

"Until the store closed, she circled the block, looking to see if there would be a different salesperson in there, so that she could go in and ask for the package. Unfortunately, it seemed that he was the only salesman on duty. So just before the store closed, she ran in and anxiously blurted out, 'Pardon me, sir, did I leave a [posterior breeze] in here?'

"She was so embarrassed that she turned around and ran out the door. She made her husband go back and get the package the next day."

Louise of St. Paul: "When I graduated from nursing school, I went to work at a large university hospital. Now, this was quite an exciting place to work for a young single person, because there were a lot of medical students and residents and interns running around.

"One day, I was assigned to an elderly woman who was in a permanent vegetative state; she had had a stroke. I had just finished her morning care when it was time for her gastric-tube feeding. I had just started her tube feeding when I was unable to control a sudden burst of flatulence.

"At that moment, and to my horror, a resident doctor who I had the hots for entered the room to see this patient. When he entered the room, he was smiling and, you know, saying hi to me—and then, the noxious fumes just stopped him in his tracks.

"The smile disappeared; his eyes began to water; and he looks at me and asks: 'Whew! Did this patient just have a bowel movement?' In a panic, I replied: 'No, but I think she's working on having one.'

"With this, Dr. Dreamboat turned on his heel and left the room."

Doctor Friendly of St. Paul: "A few years ago, I had a patient who I'm sure was the world's cutest 5-year-old. Unfortunately for Susie, I had to see her frequently for a while to deal with nasty ingrown toenails. Despite the need for unpleasant treatments, she always greeted me with a heart-melting, dimpled smile.

"One particularly hectic day, I noted that she was to be my last patient, and I looked forward to finishing the day with that smile.

"The next-to-last patient was a woman with an unusual nipple discharge, which I had to express and collect for lab analysis. I went from there directly into Susie's room, still thinking about what could be causing that breast problem. As always, Susie's face lit up, teeth and dimples flashing. I said: 'Oh, Susie, I just love having you come see me. You have the cutest nipples I've ever seen.' I instantly recognized my gaffe, and I tried to explain my brain's cross-wiring to Susie's rather startled mother.

"This was to be the last visit for the toe problem, and I never saw Susie again. I often wonder whether her mother avoided me, thinking I was some kind of secret pedophile."

Mike of St. Croix Falls, Wis.: "Last week, I went to the chiropractor, and my little girl went with me. She's 2½. I'm layin' there on the table, having my back worked on, and the chiropractor says to my daughter: 'Boy, you aren't gonna leave your daddy for anything, are you?'

"I reached out to rub her back and give her a little pat. Turned out the doctor says: 'That's me.' I'd been rubbin' his leg.

"I said I was sorry. He said: 'That's OK. It felt pretty good.' "

Steve of Woodbury: "When I'm shopping with my wife, she has a habit of stopping at a display—and without knowing she's gone, I keep walking. Not too long ago, we were walkin' through the mall and she pulled this same stunt. Now as I approached the Victoria's Secret shop—you know how it's got that sexy lingerie in there—I said: 'Oh, honey! I bet you'd look hot in that outfit.' I turned to look at her, and here was a lady that I'd never seen before in my life.

"She looked me right in the eye and said: 'In your dreams, buddy.' "

Patty of Phalen Park: "This took place in 1961, when I was being raised in a Catholic, very traditional family.

"There was a group of us girls who took a hike out behind Phalen; found a *Playboy* magazine; decided it would be a mortal sin only if we *touched* the pictures—so we used a stick to turn the pages. We went through the whole magazine and then were very remorseful, so we all decided we were going to go to confession the next day.

"There were three confessionals in the church: two in the back, which were hidden, so the priest couldn't ever see your face; the other one was down the center aisle, where the priest sat out in the open. The nun told me to go down the center aisle—in those days, they would designate, 'You go to this one, you go to that one'—and the priest looked out and saw that I was coming.

"I knelt down and said: 'Bless me, Father, for I have sinned. This is my confession'—and proceeded to tell my little, minute sins. And then I went on to say: 'And I have also committed adultery.'

"The priest said: 'Excuse me? Could you please repeat that?'

"I said: 'Father, I'm really sorry. I have committed adultery.'

"He said: 'What, exactly, did you do?'

"I said: 'Oh, Father, I looked at a dirty *Playboy* magazine—but I didn't touch it! I didn't touch it!'

"He sat back and said: 'No, my dear, you have not committed adultery.'

49

"I went: 'I haven't? Then what's adultery?'

"He said: 'You go home and ask your mother.'

"When I asked my mother and she told me, I was so embarrassed that every time I ever saw this priest at our parish, I would look the other way. He always had this grin on his face, knowing that I was the silly little sixth-grade girl who thought that adultery was looking at dirty pictures."

Lisa of St. Paul: "One of my part-time jobs is to work for a well-known wine store here in the Cities, and I once had a customer in the store who told me she was looking for a wine for a dinner party.

"As we were talking, she mentioned that she had been trying to find an ingredient to go in a mushroom soup recipe that she had. When I asked her what it was, explaining that I also love to cook, she said she was looking for dry sherry. I said: 'Well, come this way!'

"I took her down the aisle and handed her a bottle of Spanish dry sherry—and she said: 'Oh, don't I feel stupid! The people at Lund's must think I'm crazy. I've been looking for the *powdered* kind.' "

Lisa's Sister of Frederic, Wis.: "About a year ago, Lisa called my dad to say hello. She said: 'Hi, how ya doin'?' He said: 'Fine.'

"She said: 'So what are you up to, Dad?' And he said: 'I'm sittin' here eatin' birthday cake.'

"She said: 'Really? Well, whose birthday is it?' And he said: 'It's mine.' "

Beryl of St. Paul: "My husband has the habit of reading or doing crosswords in the bathroom. In fact, I even put a magazine rack in there. Just now, I entered the bathroom and found a fairly difficult, completed crossword on top of the rack.

" 'Oh!' I said. 'Did you do all that?'

" 'Oh, Lordy!' came the answer. 'Did I forget to flush?'

Mary Sue of Mahtomedi: "One of my simple pleasures is to find a letter in the mailbox from Aunt Marion, who is retired out in Arizona. She always includes entertaining anecdotes.

"For example, from the most recent letter: 'One of our friends said that when she and her husband first came to Arizona, they played a lot of golf. She decided she should have a nice golfing outfit, so she found one: a white top and a skirt with a very small blue scatter print, which she wore happily. They both graduated from college in Minnesota, and went back for a class reunion. She wore her golf outfit to one of the events, still quite happy with it. A few days later, they visited their nephew, and he said, puzzled: 'Nancy, how come you have that skirt with the word "s—" printed all over it?' "

A.J. of St. Paul: "My mother weaves rag rugs, and quite often she goes to garage sales, buys old sheets, tears them up for rags. One day, she found a good deal on some sheets at a garage sale, went home, washed them, hung them outside to dry—and eventually did a double take at one of the sheets.

"Turns out the whole sheet was covered with silhouettes of a couple having sex in just about every imaginable position—and even some that are tough to imagine."

Irvin of Lino Lakes: "Last year, my wife wanted to buy one of the Christmas trees at our local Tom Thumb store. There was a lot of snow, and the trees stood in the snowbank. She sent me inside to pay for it.

"I came back out to put it in the car, and it seemed to be stuck in the snowbank. I pulled and pulled on it; it seemed to be frozen down. She got out and helped me. We couldn't pull it out, either one of us, and it was the only one she wanted.

"So we went in to get our money back from the clerk, and he suggested that he would come out and shovel it out for us or help us pull it out. We said: 'No. That's OK. Just give us the money back.'

"Last spring when the snow was gone, we went by there, and we could see that that particular tree was planted in the ground—and is growing very nicely even yet. We laugh about it every time we go by there."

John of St. Paul: "For years, my buddy and I fished a lot together. Our favorite bait for the one-pound sunnies was an angleworm and a piece of corn. My buddy said: 'Be sure to get a can of corn.' So that night, I went to the store and picked up a can of corn.

"We got out on the lake the next morning, ready to fish. My buddy asked if I'd got the corn. I said: 'Yep.' He said: 'Well, hand it over.' Guess what. Instead of whole-kernel corn, I'd grabbed a can of creamed corn.

"Ever try to put creamed corn on a fish hook? Doesn't work very well."

Merlyn of St. Paul: "Several years ago, my family and I traveled out East. I had a trade show to do; my husband had a college reunion. We decided to call the rest a camping vacation.

"We drove through upper Michigan and across Canada, rather than tackle

51

Chicago. On our first day out, we drove until dark and then started looking for a place to stay. No camping that night.

"We settled for a small strip motel, probably built before World War II, along the highway. It had a little café attached, so we got something there for supper and retired for the night. The coffee was *not* great, so we vowed to make our own in the morning to take with us on the road.

"Morning came. We wanted to get on the road fast, so while showers were being taken, we set up our good old camping coffeepot and hot plate. The only place in the room where there was an electric outlet was behind the aging TV set, so the hot plate had to sit on the TV.

"Halfway through our packing, the TV was on to some morning show— and it started crackling. I looked up and saw the hot plate and the coffee slowly tip to one side and sink into the TV set, dumping the pot's contents inside the TV.

"I yanked both electric cords and sat there watching coffee drip out of the bottom of the TV. As my husband exited the shower, he had the good sense to throw his towels down on the rug to sop up our mess. But the damage was done: We had melted the TV.

"We tipped the TV over to drain out the coffee, but from the big hole in the top of the TV, we knew it was dead. As we stared at it, the conversation went something like 'Well, who put it there, anyway?' and 'How did *I* know it would melt?' and 'What do we tell them when we check out?' and '*You* tell them!' and 'No, *you* tell them!'

"I finally chickened and made my husband check out, alone. He told them, apologetically, and left his VISA card number to charge us for the damages.

"At the next K mart we passed on the road, we squealed to a halt, bought a new hot plate and pitched the old culprit in their garbage can.

"A charge never came through for the damages, thanks to the kindness of the motel owner. I guess in her business, she had seen stranger vandals than us—but none more embarrassed."

Dan of Arden Hills: "When I was 19, I worked at Disney World in Florida driving the submarines in '20,000 Leagues Under the Sea.' The submarines traveled on a track, and on busy days the submarines in the back would be held up in a given area while the submarines up front were loading and unloading passengers. Invariably, we would be stuck in what we called 'The Octopus Section,' which was a scene showing an octopus guarding treasure. People would wonder why we were stopped.

"I was instructed to get on the microphone and say, 'Ladies and gentlemen, there has been a slight delay. Apparently, one of the octopus' tentacles has been wrapped up in a propeller. We're sending divers to straighten it out.'

"But one time, I don't know what I was thinking, because I said, 'Ladies and gentlemen, there is going to be a slight delay. Apparently, one of the octopus' testicles is wrapped up in our propeller.' I couldn't show my face as people were unloading."

Woody of Lilydale: "Years ago, when my daughter Susie was a child, she had a G.I. Joe doll. One night, she came to me to complain that the doll was broken. Sure enough, the doll's legs were dangling down from the body.

"I looked it over and determined that there was a plastic pin molded into the doll's stomach, and it was broken—allowing the rubber binder holding the legs to the body of the doll to be loose and flopping about.

"Well, being a typical father, I promised Susie I would fix it—then set it aside and promptly forgot about it.

"Some time later, I was in a department store, near the toy department, and I noticed a G.I. Joe doll on display. That jolted my memory about the broken doll, and I thought that as long as I was in the store, I might just as well check out the display doll—to see if my diagnosis was correct.

"So I picked it up and pulled Joe's G.I. pants down. Just then, this cute little clerk walked up wearing that 'Can I help you?' smile—but that smile turned pretty sickly when she looked down and saw what I was doing.

"I wanted to say: 'No, no, no. It's not what you think. I can *explain!*' But I never had the chance; she walked right by me. Perhaps she felt like screaming and running by.

"Me, I just pulled Joe's pants back up and got the hell out of there."

CHAPTER 7

Lovers and Friends

First love: From **Terri** of Cottage Grove:

"When I was about 4 years old, I really loved our garbage man. He was a really nice guy; he always talked to us when he picked up the garbage. I looked forward to seeing him each week—and I even have a photograph of him and me outside our house.

"One day, I thought I would surprise him: Instead of seeing garbage, garbage, garbage all day long, I thought I'd fill the 30-gallon can with some pretty white sand from our backyard. It took me almost all day to do it, with just my bucket and little shovel.

"Well, my labor of love didn't work out so well—because I think I probably gave the man a hernia when he tried to lift it. It's funny: We didn't see our favorite garbage man for weeks afterwards."

And now **Elaine** of White Bear: "My 5-year-old kindergarten daughter had the biggest crush on her school-bus driver, a young man named Mike. Apparently, several of her little girlfriends felt the same. This went on for several months, with my daughter proclaiming that she was going to be a bus driver when she grew up.

"One day, I realized that she hadn't mentioned Mike in quite a while, so I asked her about him. She said: 'We don't like him anymore.' And when I asked her why, she said: 'He picks his nose.' And that was that."

A simple smile: From **Mary** of St. Paul:

"I was swinging my little niece Natalie the other day. Natalie was swinging next to a little boy who couldn't be more than 4 years old; she's 3. The little boy was so happy to be loving his daddy, who was swinging him, and he started to talk about his love for his daddy. He said: 'I *love* my daddy, and I *love* my mommy.' And my dear little Natalie, whose father died two years ago of leukemia, turned to him on the swing and said: 'I love my mommy—but my daddy already died.'

54

"I didn't know what to say. And the little boy responded *perfectly*—with just a smile toward her—as the two adults pushing these profound children had no idea what to say. He took care of it for dear Natalie. Children somehow, even at 3 years of age, can support each other, where adults don't know what to do."

Young love: The sweet-voiced **Amy** of the St. Croix Valley:

"The other day, my boyfriend and I were talking—and out of the blue, he says to me: 'Do you need to be 18 to buy condoms?' He said it really serious-like, and I said to him: 'No, you have to be 21.' And he said: 'Are you *serious?*'

"I thought it was the funniest thing in the world. It was so cute. He's so innocent. I love him so much."

The course of true love: From **Jimbo** of St. Paul:

"A college friend of mine told me that the first time he had his heart truly broken, he was extremely depressed for a year—almost to the point of catatonia.

"He finally emerged from it and met another True Love; she also gave him the boot—and once again, he was *extremely* depressed. But the second time, it only lasted a month.

"He got over her, went out with another woman; she gave him the boot—and again, equally depressed. The third time, it only lasted a week.

"I guess this guy got to the point where a woman could spit on him, treat him like utter trash, and he could go in his room and be by himself for five minutes of depression—and emerge perfectly happy."

Hope springs eternal: A message of hope for a heartbroken woman named Becky, who asked B. Boarders for tales of even better love the next time around, from an **anonymous woman:**

"A few years ago, the man I was in love with left me for another woman that I later found out he'd been seeing the entire time we were together. I pretty much fell apart after that; I hadn't realized how much I loved him.

"That fall, I met my husband—a really great man who makes me feel like the most beautiful woman in the world. We've been married two years in March, and we have a gorgeous little boy.

"I hear from my friends now that my ex is a nasty-looking bum with no home. The other woman dumped him a month after he left me—so there really is a God."

Just say no: An observation by **Cindy** of Highland Park:

"It's my belief that *abstinence* makes the heart grow fonder—and the miles don't have too much to do with it."

What lovers do: Ritual attractions:

Fiamma of Forest Lake: "Whenever my husband gets home late at night and comes in the door, he goes: 'Meoo?' *[BULLETIN BOARD CLARIFIES, because the letters of the English language cannot be organized to convey this sound properly: It's the sound of a shy little baby cat saying, "Is my mama around here someplace?"]* If he doesn't go 'Meoo' and I hear a door, I get real scared.

"The other thing we always do: When he leaves in the morning, I look through the window and we do the sign for 'I love you' in American Sign Language, which is . . . here we go: Take your right hand; make a fist, with the back of your hand toward you; put your thumb out; put your index finger up and your little finger up—and you have shorthand for 'I love you.'

"And oh, I forgot. One other thing: We still hold hands, even though we're a couple of old fogies. I hold his middle two fingers when we're walking. It feels better; it just fits."

Navasanki of St. Paul: "My boyfriend has a cat. I wasn't experienced with cats when I started going out with him, and I noticed his cat did something kind of strange. When she was sitting there bread-loaf-style, with her feet all tucked in, and she decided she liked you a lot, she'd reach out and poke you with her paw. Just kind of poke you a little bit. He said that stemmed from when she was younger; she used to tap people in the face to wake them up, to let them know it was time to feed her. He told me it was just her way of saying that she loved me.

"I know this is a nauseatingly cute story—but whenever we try to say we love each other, we reach out and touch each other, you know, on the chest, in the middle there. I like it a lot; it's always reassuring when he does that."

Funny Valentine: From an **anonymous woman:**

"The few times that my husband and I tried something new, it backfired to the point where we ended up looking like Lucy Ricardo and Ethel Mertz in the candy factory.

"A decade ago, I purchased a bottle of Emotion Lotion. It looked like bright-red salad oil, but it smelled and tasted like cinnamon red-hots. You know, those little candies? I plopped that little bottle on the table on St. Valentine's Day and awaited the arrival of my loved one. When he came home, he brought me—yawn—the flowers and chocolates.

"As I was arranging my posies, I heard an anguished cry. I rushed to the source and found my husband knee-deep in paperwork; that darned red-hot Emotion Lotion bottle had somehow leaked all over our income-tax stuff that he had slaved over for days and days. We installed a makeshift clothesline over our bathtub and deferred Cupid's holiday.

"Later, we obtained new forms for *some* of it, but to this day, we both giggle about the documents drenched in that stuff—and wonder what the IRS person must have thought."

To know him is to love him: From **Just Kim** of St. Paul:

"My simple pleasure is that I gave somebody that I love a simple pleasure.

"I went out Saturday night, so I was kinda draggin' Sunday. And after my boyfriend put plastic on my windows and we ate dinner, we lounged out on the couch. I was laying against his chest, watching TV, and my cat crawled up on the other side of his chest.

"Well, the next thing I know, I wake up and two hours have passed. I couldn't believe the man did not move for two hours, so he wouldn't wake either of us. He actually said it was two of the most wonderful hours he's spent, content to be cuddled by his two favorite girls.

"What a guy! You gotta love him, huh?"

BULLETIN BOARD REPLIES: No, Just Kim. But it appears you'd be a fool not to.

To know him is to have him love you: From **Tried and True** of St. Paul:

"I received a mail-order classical-music compact disc the other day, and I noticed that the pianist accompanying the singer happens to share my first and last names. Since I do play the piano, I mischievously decided to see if I could trick my girlfriend of six months into believing I had performed on the album.

"The next time I saw her, I showed her the CD and said: 'Look what the record company sent me! I recorded this back in college. I didn't know they were going to reissue it.'

"Girlfriend (smiling sarcastically): 'Yeah, right.'

"Me (with my best feigned hurt look): 'What's the matter? Don't you believe I can play the piano that well?'

"Girlfriend: 'I'm sure you can. What I *don't* believe is that you could have gone six months without bragging about it.'

"You've gotta love a woman like that."

Faint praise: The news from Corn Dog Corner (a Corn Dog being "an insult wrapped in a compliment," as defined by **Muriel** of Chippewa Falls, Wis.):

Nancy of East Bethel: "When I was 18 years old and dancing with my first boyfriend—romantically, to 'Color My World'—we were the only ones in my family's house, in the basement, and he looked at me so seriously and said: 'Right now, you look . . . so . . . homely.' I knew what he meant, but I don't think he knew what he meant."

Phoebe of St. Paul: "My husband and me and a friend were playing Trivial Pursuit. The friend really didn't want to play; she thought you needed to know a lot. But we talked her into it, and it ended up that she won.

"I said to her: 'See, you don't have to be smart to win Trivial Pursuit.' Dumb, huh?"

The Mother of Six of Hastings: "I had just pulled out some freshly baked Macadamia-nut white-chocolate cookies. (They're fantastic.) And a friend of mine stopped by. I gave her a couple of 'em, because she's a Macadamia-nut fanatic. She looked at me, and she said: 'You know, it's amazing that you're not fatter than you are, with these kind of cookies in the house.' And then she left! I don't even think she knew what she said."

R.W. of Maplewood: "Talk about faint praise! I was talking to a friend on the phone today, and she told me that there's an ad for a plus-size model search in today's paper and that I should make an appointment because modeling pays big bucks. I said: 'No. You might not have to be thin, but you've gotta be really gorgeous.' And she goes: 'Nah. The woman in the ad is a lot uglier than you are.' "

Sassy of St. Paul: "A long time ago, my friend Linda and I, after spending a very hot and humid day at the Minnesota State Fair, collapsed on the living-room floor in my apartment and shed our clothes while waiting for my air conditioner to crank up.

"Linda, who was on the plump side, peeked over at me and said what a nice shape I had. I was smilin', and gettin' ready to thank her, when she blurted out: 'Gee, if only I could have your bod! But I'd want to keep my own face, of course.' "

Kathy of Eagan: "One day, I brought my 2-year-old daughter to a baby shower. The next day, my co-worker was telling me that my daughter was so cute—how sweet it was that she can say 'Please,' 'Thank you,' 'Excuse me.'

"Then my co-worker says to me: 'You must have a really good baby-sitter.' "

Katie of Stillwater: "I have a friend who knew that I had a twin sister, but she had never met her. One day, she said to me: 'You know, I thought I saw your twin sister at the mall yesterday—but then I realized she was way too pretty to be your twin.' "

"Come to think of it, I guess that wasn't really a faint-praise story at all. There was no praise in it."

Dating in the '90s: From **Leah** of Minneapolis:

"My husband and I were enjoying dinner in Minneapolis Friday evening when another couple sat down behind us. I couldn't see them, but I could overhear their conversation, and I would tune in and out. He was probably about 50, and she was probably about 40—and they obviously had been dating for only a month or so. A couple of the excerpts were really quite humorous:

"First of all, I caught her saying: 'I live on the edge.' And then, a slight pause as she rethought that, and she said: 'Well, actually I live on the *edge* of the edge.'

"Later on, I caught her asking him how many women he had slept with. He kind of hemmed and hawed around the subject, and she really pushed him to give her a figure. She said: 'I'm just concerned that you don't remember how many.'

"He said: 'I remember how many. It's just from the look on your face, I can tell that there's a good number and a bad number.'

"I thought that was rather funny."

And from **David** of South Minneapolis:

"Early this year, I met this really nice guy at work—real cute little guy. He ended up asking me if I'd go with him to the '90s [*full name: The Gay '90s— and with good reason*]—'cause he'd never been there before. I was pretty certain this guy was straight, so I was really kinda confused what was going on. But we agreed to make final arrangements later on that night.

"Got home, called this guy, we made final arrangements—and then I hung up the phone and just screeched out, real loud: 'What am I *doing*? I'm going to The Gay '90s with a straight man who's 14 years younger than me on the day I get a prescription for bifocals!'

"One of my roommates was in the living room, and he sort of jumped three feet when I exploded like that. He looked at me and said: 'Sounds perfectly normal for this place.'

"So we went out, and I just kinda watched him to see how he reacted. He just wanted, basically, to go to the '90s.

"The next day, I was talking to a friend at work who's also gay, and he said: 'You know, we've got a word for people like that—for straight men like that.'

"I said: 'Yeah, I think we call them friends.'"

59

The buddy system: From **Linda W.** of Eagan:

"I have to tell you what happened to my little boy. Jay is 7, and yesterday, he was playing with his friend Nick, who's also 7, and Nick accidentally hit Jay right between the eyes with his hockey stick. Jay got a bloody nose and was crying so hard; he's got a couple good shiners.

"This morning, Nick brought him a little gift, a book, and he had a card made out for him that said: 'Jay, I'm sorry for hitting your face.'

"His mom said to him: 'How did you feel, Nick, when that happened to Jay?' And Nick said: 'I coulda barfed my heart out.' That's friendship for you."

The buddy system (II): From **Curt** of parts unknown:

"Dumbest thing I've ever done: My friend talked me into joinin' the Army with him. The buddy system, right? He says: 'It's gonna be great! We get free education—free everything, you know? It's not too bad; it's not gonna be that hard.' So we go over and take our physicals, and he's all gung-ho about joinin' the Army. 'This is gonna be great,' he says.

"Well, we got separated the last day of our physicals and testing and that kind of stuff; I went ahead and finished up my stuff. I took my oath and was ready to go in the Army. Went back to the hotel.

"He came in, and I said: 'Well, how 'bout that! We joined the Army, huh?' He says: 'No, we didn't join the Army. *You* did. I changed my mind. I'm goin' home.' I went off to the Army; he went home. Pretty dumb, huh?"

Best friends: From **Plain Jane** of the West Side:

"This summer, I drove to Illinois to visit my best friend, Tia, so we could celebrate 25 years of friendship by spending a few days visiting old friends and haunts.

"As a small gift, I brought along a pair of patchwork pot holders that I had bought, for $3, at the St. Paul farmers' market. They were quite lovely, but obviously not a big deal.

"That evening, while we were cooking supper, one of the pot holders got too close to the gas burner and caught fire. It was quickly extinguished, but the pot holder was a little worse for wear. Since Tia already had a sizable collection of burned pot holders, I didn't think she needed another, so I wanted her to throw it in the trash—but Tia wouldn't hear of it.

"The next morning, I took the burned pot holder and put it in my purse—so that I could give it back to her in case she made *too* big of a stink. She almost instantly noticed that the pot holder was missing. I lied and told her that I'd put it in the trash before it was collected that morning. Well, she was *furious* with me. *[BULLETIN BOARD INTERJECTS: What are best friends for, if not to get furious with about a buck-and-a-half pot holder?]*

"I finally said to her something that I'd heard her say to her 3½-year-old son during one of his spells: 'It's OK for you to be angry with me, but I still love you.'

"It took some time, but I think she's forgiven me. If not, I hope she will when she gets her Christmas present from me this year: the burned pot holder, nicely matted and framed, with the inscription 'It's OK for you to be angry with me, but I still love you.' "

CHAPTER 8

Husbands and Wives

Stories of the married life:

Annals of male insecurity: From **The Husband** of St. Paul:
"So we're home from the honeymoon—blissfully, radiantly in love. I'm helping her move her stuff into my place. Mundane cleaning and unpacking seem like romantic interludes, because we're doing them together.

"She's unpacking boxes of old clothes that have been in storage, unused for years; she has to decide what to keep, what to give to Goodwill, what to throw away. Most items are going into the Goodwill pile—until she pulls out one unmistakably 1970s-style dress. A warm, nostalgic smile crosses her face.

" 'Oh, I couldn't give *this* away,' she says, in the kind of voice people reserve for describing an adorable puppy. 'This is the dress I was wearing the night I lost my virginity!' "

And then again, later, it's **The Husband** of St. Paul: "On the eve of our four-month wedding anniversary, I asked my new bride whether she was still happy to have married me. I was expecting a few cheap, positive, emotional strokes in return. Instead I got this:

" 'Well, sort of. I've moved out of the phase of thinking that this was the biggest mistake of my life into the phase of thinking that I've done it, so I might as well make the best of it.' "

Annals of female insecurity: Filed by **[Anonymous Woman]** of somewhere:
"A few years ago, I was taking some of my husband's clothes out of the dryer when I found what appeared to be a condom. My husband and I had never used condoms, so I was understandably upset.

"I called my sister, sobbing, saying I would never have suspected my husband of having an affair. We decided I needed to approach him as soon as he got home.

62

"So when he did, he could tell something was wrong right away and asked me about it. Thrusting my finger at the thing lying on the counter, I said: 'Would you care to explain *that?*'

"Calm as can be, he says: 'Yeah. You put it on your finger to make it easier to turn pages or count money.'

"Angrier now, I say: 'You expect me to believe that?'

"A slow grin spreads across his face, and he says: 'You think that's a *condom,* don't you?'

"By this time, I'm stunned into silence and beginning to wonder. '[Anonymous Woman],' he says, 'don't you think it's kind of *small* to be a condom?'

"Redder in the face by the moment, I reply, 'I thought it shrunk in the dryer.'

" 'Rubber doesn't shrink, [Anonymous Woman].' "

Faint praise: More from Corn Dog Corner:

Virginia of St. Paul: "My husband, every once in a while—not very often—will say: 'Boy, you look cute this morning.'

"And then he'll say: 'What's the deal?' "

Mac of Mollygrove: "I'm expecting a baby in a few months, and the other day I was feeling insecure about my changing body, not feeling very attractive. My husband, in a sincere attempt to silence my fears, said: 'Oh, honey, you're not any more unattractive than you were before you were pregnant.'

"I knew what he meant, but . . .' "

Barb W. of Oakdale: "Last night, my husband complimented me on a household-repair job that I had done. Feigning modesty, I said: 'It was no big deal. Any idiot could have done it.' Then I qualified: 'Well, maybe not *any* idiot.'

"His reply? 'My idiot can!' Gee, thanks—I think."

The Pathfinder of Shoreview: "My beautiful wife has been talking about the Bulletin Board and saying: 'Have you noticed that they seem to like to print stuff of a semi-intellectual nature?'

"I said: 'Yeah, I've noticed that.'

"She says: 'Well, *we're* that kind of people.'

"I think I've just been insulted. I think she just called me a half-wit."

Funny what we remember . . . and don't: From **Beth** of Woodbury:

"We got together with friends on New Year's Day, and the talk eventually led to golf.

"My husband, Jeff, was relating—shot by shot—some golf hole on some golf course he played 10 years ago. The other guys were enthralled—and would also relive some great game, recalling exact scores on each hole: 'Yeah, I shot par, par, bogey, birdie, double bogey, etc., etc., on the back side.' And: 'Oh, remember No. 13? With the dogleg to the right and the pine grove on the left.'

"Now, I love golf, too, and play frequently, but I don't recall every club I use on every hole, nor the exact yardage, nor the condition of the greens, nor the trouble spots of each hole, nor my slices and fades for that day. I *might* remember my total score.

"Well . . . recently, I asked Jeff where he put the stapler a day ago. He looked at me with a blank stare. He didn't have a clue.

"I find the difference in the selective memories of men and women to be . . . peculiar.

"Carpe diem."

Modern Romance: From **JB's Wife** (whose Bulletin Board handle might suggest a subservience that is nowhere evident in the stories she tells):

"JB isn't exactly an extravagant or creative kind of guy, but I never give up hope that *this* Valentine's Day will be different.

"As soon as we woke up on Sunday morning, we decided to exchange gifts. JB was pretty happy with himself that he had a card and gift waiting for me— and considering his track record, I was, too. So I opened the card, and it was pretty nice. He told me that Rachel (our 10-year-old daughter) helped pick it out.

"Then I opened the bag to see what my present was, and I found two $100,000 candy bars and a Baby Ruth. I told him, 'I bet you got these at the store, three for a dollar.'

"He got a funny look on his face, and Rachel started giggling. Then she confessed: 'Mom, they were really four for a dollar, but we ate one in the car.'

"Well, maybe next year . . ."

Dept. of Affectionate Marital Ridicule: And here, once again, is **JB's Wife**:

"Last year for my birthday, JB made me an angel-food cake that was kind of flat. He didn't know where we kept the electric mixer, so he used the blender instead! When the batter kept expanding, powder started shooting out the top like Old Faithful and the batter spilled over the edges of the blender, all over the counter. So JB simply poured it back in the mixing bowl and beat the daylights out of it with a wooden spoon.

"This year's cake was pretty good. I must admit that I was a little worried, because the directions on the box said 'Grease the pan,' and he asked me: 'Just the inside?' "

Every time is an occasion: From **Lynne** of Stacy:

"I was just going to let you know about this great cake recipe I got this spring. It's called the Better Than Sex Cake, and I've been making it for every occasion: birthdays, baptisms, Father's Day, everything.

"My husband was laughing the other day as I was making this cake for another occasion, and we decided to rename it the More Often Than Sex Cake."

Touché! From an **anonymous man:**

"My wife and I were recently considering my getting a vasectomy. We've got two children, and we seem to be fairly content. Why tempt fate with more children that we don't necessarily want or can afford?

"I went to the doctor for the screening, and he gave me the literature, and I brought it home to my wife; she was reading it, and she said: 'Boy, this is kinda final, isn't it?'

"My response was—sorry about the vulgarity, but: 'No s— !' So I had to call and cancel my appointment.

"I spoke with the nurse and said: 'I'm canceling my appointment for the vasectomy' on such-and-such a date. And she said: 'OK.' I just had to; I said: 'I bet you have a lot of cancellations, don't you?'

"She said: 'Yes, we do.'

"My response was: 'Well, my wife was intimidated by the finality of it, and she decided to go with a Norplant.'

"The nurse responded: 'Yeah, and they've all got an *excuse*, too.' "

Company's coming: From **Jean** of Mahtomedi:

"We had a neighborhood party, and all our neighbors were gonna come over and get to know one another. So I cleaned the house—and we have two bathrooms, so I did the upstairs bathroom and told my husband that if he could help out and clean the downstairs bathroom, it would help a lot.

"Well, my job took maybe half an hour; my husband was done in 10 minutes. I went downstairs, and the bathroom was really clean—except that I noticed in the soap dish . . . you know how you put out little pretty soaps for your guests, or at least a nice clean bar for them? I noticed this . . . mound shaped into a bar. It was a mound of . . . I didn't know quite what it was. It was a mound of soap—and he was so *proud* that he had collected all the little soaps from around the house and squished it into one big bar for our guests to use.

"I left it as it was, 'cause he was really proud of it, and nobody said anything about it—but, you know, that's husbands."

Bonnie of West St. Paul: "Just one sentence: My husband is the first guest to arrive."

Annals of anal retentiveness: From **Joanie** of Lakeville:

"My ex-husband used to fold four or five sheets of toilet paper into a little stack, and then he'd stack his little stacks on the back seat of the toilet. I was not supposed to touch those, but one day we ran out and I really had no choice.

"I figured I could just run out, get the toilet paper and replace 'em—and he'd never know! So I did that. I folded 'em up all up. The height was just about the same; it was the exact-same toilet paper, the exact-same color.

"He came home, glanced in the bathroom and said: 'You used my toilet paper.' He *knew* because he folded the sheets a specific way, so that the edges were just at the right angle or something!

"But . . . he's, as I said, my ex-husband. Need I say more?"

And from **Liz** of White Bear Lake: "When my husband started traveling for his business, 27 years ago, I packed his suitcase for the first trip. Before closing it, I had noticed him anxiously watching, pacing and biting his nails. He asked if I minded if he repacked it. I said no, I didn't mind—then stood by as he rearranged his undershirts and briefs so all of the Fruit of the Loom labels pointed the same direction.

"Needless to say, I have not packed his suitcase in the subsequent 27 years of traveling."

The phantom: From **M.N.** of parts undisclosed:

"Shortly after my husband and I got married, about 19 years ago, I discovered that I would go to bed with him and wake up with someone else.

"At least a couple of times a week, in the middle of the night, he'd roll over and call my name—real low and sexy-like. He'd get *extremely* passionate. He'd look right at me and talk to me, and it was always *so* romantic—but in the morning, he'd rarely remember having done it! Occasionally, when I'd bring it up to him, he'd remember, and then he'd be genuinely embarrassed. In fact, the whole situation still embarrasses him, but I love it.

"I've told him that as I see it, it means that his love for me is so deep that it's even in his subconscious.

"We now refer to this nocturnal visitor as the Phantom, and on the mornings after his visits, all I have to say is: 'Honey, the Phantom struck again.'

And my poor hubby can do nothing but roll his eyes, shake his head and blush. He is so sweet, and it is so wonderful.

"So I want to say: I love you, N.B.; those are his initials."

BULLETIN BOARD REPLIES: Thank God for that. Would've been a heckuva punch line, any other way.

Say it with flowers! A memoir by **That Woman** of Northfield:

"Many years ago, my husband wanted to plant some crocuses in our backyard. We lived in Illinois then. He asked: 'Where shall I plant them?' And I said: 'Just take a handful, throw them out in the yard, and plant them wherever they land.'

"But he had a mathematical engineer's mind, and he couldn't do that.

"In the spring, I looked out from our second-floor living-room window, into our back yard, and read 'I LOVE YOU' in purple and white crocuses."

I do, I do: From **Linda W.** of Eagan:

"I just celebrated my birthday. My husband surprised me by taking me out for dinner—and before we went to Forepaugh's, one of our very special places, he stopped on the High Bridge overlook, where he'd proposed to me.

"We were looking at the city, and he said: 'I want to know if you'll stay married to me.'

"I said: 'What? What do you mean?'

"He said: 'Will you stay married to me?' I just looked at him—and he gave me the most gorgeous sapphire-and-diamond ring for my birthday. I love him, and it was one of the sweetest things he ever did for me. And he had a long-stemmed red rose delivered to the restaurant, and we had a wonderful dinner together.

"He is just sweet."

CHAPTER 9

All in the Family

On the joys and pains of family life:

Plant a jelly bean, and watch it grow: From **Annie, Jesse James, Tuffy, Toto and Doodlebug**:

"Jelly beans remind us of more than just Easter. They bring back memories of our wonderful grandpa Leo Pierson and his extraordinary jelly-bean garden.

"On that early-spring morning 10 years ago, as our grandpa led us to the backyard, he explained that if you plant a jelly bean and water it every day, a lollipop will soon grow in its place.

"He handed us each a different-colored jelly bean, which he then instructed us to carefully place in the holes which he had dug. Gently we dropped our jelly beans in and covered them with dirt. After sprinkling water on the mounds, we sat transfixed for hours, waiting for the first signs of life from our lollipop seeds.

"Faithfully we watered and cared for our garden, and soon our efforts paid off: There, where jelly beans had been, stood five lollipop sticks. We were delighted that they had sprouted, and Grandpa assured us that they would bloom soon.

"Sure enough, on Easter Sunday, we ran to the backyard to find five brightly colored lollipops sticking up out of the ground. We called Grandpa to help us harvest our crop, and soon we were happily licking away on our lollipops.

"Grandpa is no longer with us to carry on this tradition, but we hope that other grandpas will become jelly-bean gardeners, too.

"We love you and miss you, Grandpa."

Third time's . . . not quite the charm: From **Tim Casey** of Eagan:

"Over the years, I've found that the joy of finding out that you are going to be a dad again diminishes over time—not only for you, but also for your spouse.

"With our first child, it was: 'Tim! We're pregnant! Hello, *Daddy*!'

"With our second one, it was a Saturday morning, and she laid a box of pink booties on my chest while I was sleeping and said: 'Think pink.' And it turned out to be a girl.

"The third one: We found out not too long ago; my wife comes in the door and says: 'You want to look at minivans?'

"Well, I guess that's just part of life."

Dawn of the living brain-dead: From **Pam** of St. Paul:

"I'm a mom, and the other day I was sitting down to a nice dinner that my husband had made—and I started cutting up all my food into tiny, little pieces, just like you would for a 1-year-old. I suddenly stopped and realized what I was doing. That was kind of depressing."

Help wanted! From an **anonymous woman:**

"Forget phone sex. I need 1-900-MOMMIES.

"A soothing voice on the other end of the telephone reminding me that childhood is short, they are only with us for a while; maybe a video-phone setup that will show me photos of my children at their shining best.

"I need a number to dial on those mornings when I've written checks to the school for candy bars that were supposed to be sold, not eaten; for those mornings when the door is closed after the last kid leaves and I turn around to face the debris from a family that mistakes the floor for a shelf and a wastebasket; for those mornings when I wash more cups, glasses and towels than I ever remember owning.

"I need someone to tell me that I will miss those little voices calling each other names, fighting over *anything*, whining about 'It's not fair!'

"A 900 number that I can call for a little reassurance, to set me back on the right path.

"Better make that an 800 number. I think we ate too many candy bars again."

Today's helpful hint: It's from **The Happy Homemaker** of Mahtomedi:

"This is for anybody else who spends their life matching and folding socks.

"It gets a little tedious after eight or 10 years, folding socks for five pairs of feet—so I decided to start thinking about socks as something to go on feet that I really love. You've just gotta think about those little feet when they first emerged from your body, when they were born, and about their little toes curled up at night in their beds.

"If you think about socks that way, it goes a lot faster."

Clever Parent Tricks: From **Bud** of North Branch:

"My sons David and Matt went to hockey camp with Steve, and Steve's mother told him: 'Be sure you brush your teeth every day, Steve.' Steve's mom and Jan *[Bud's wife, we're guessing]* and I went to pick up the boys after hockey camp, and Steve's mom said: 'Well, Steve, how are your teeth? Did you brush them every day?'

" 'Certainly, Mom!'

"Mom said: 'Could I see your toothbrush, please?'

"He handed her his toothbrush, which was still in the case—and that's fine; that's where it should be. She opened the case, and around the handle unfurled the neatest $10 bill you ever saw in your life."

Cuisine comique: A culinary fiasco remembered by **Dave** of the East Side:

"Many years ago, when my sister and I were 10 or 12 years old, we decided to make some scratch brownies. We ended up putting in too much sugar— and the only way to counter that, by our reasoning, was to add an equivalent amount of salt. When things were all said and done, we ended up with brownies that were so salty that my mother was the only one who could stand to eat 'em. That says a lot for motherhood, I think."

Chivalry lives! From **Lynn** of Roseville:

"My daughter was grocery shopping with my grandson, who was 3 at the time. She filled her cart and got into the proper line. No one was in the express lane, so one of the girls motioned her over.

"Halfway through checking out, a man came behind her in line and loudly started crabbing about people with too many items. She explained that she'd been told to come into that lane—but he just kept ragging and complaining.

"Finally, my 3-year-old grandson yelled at this man: 'Leave my mama alone, you big, dumb stupidhead!' And that took care of it. Stopped the tirade."

The next time around: From **Auntie Slick** of Spooner, Wis.:

"Last night, as I was tucking my children in bed, my youngest, Dennis (age 3) gets into a discussion about what happens to us when we die. Dean (age 5½) says: 'You go to heaven when you die, and you never come back again.'

"Which prompted me to say: 'Yes, we believe that we go to heaven when we die, but some people believe that we come back to Earth if God decides we still have other things to do.'

"I thought that this was far above their heads, but as usual, Dean trumps the mommy. He says to me: 'Mom, if I come back again, can I choose you to be my mom again?'

"I just about cried. I gave him a hug and a kiss and said I hoped so."

Am I an orphan now? From **LaVonne** of Coon Rapids:

"When I was not quite 7 years old, my just-divorced mother sent me to camp, apparently thinking I would appreciate the favor. (She may also have needed the time to herself, now that I think of it.) As soon as I got there, I started bawling. I wanted to go home, and no kid or counselor could get me out of the cabin to try any of the activities.

"Finally, after a couple of days of sobbing, I heard the words I wanted to hear: 'Your mother is coming to get you today.' I was overjoyed. The camp counselors must have taken pity on me and called Mom, I thought, and she loved me enough to rescue me!

"A big, black car drove up at last, with some men I didn't know in the front seat. Mom was in the back. After a big hug, I snuggled up with her for the long ride home. I thanked her profusely for saving me from that awful camp—and then she told me the real reason she had come: My father had died.

"I started crying again. I was very young, and I didn't know my father very well, so I'm afraid the news of his death was not what upset me so much. I was broken-hearted to realize that my mother would have let me stay away from her for the camp's full two weeks if this hadn't happened. Then, re-membering a movie I had seen about an orphan that became a prince, I sniffed hopefully.

" 'Does this mean I'm an orphan now?'

" 'Oh, no, no,' said my mother, hugging me tighter. 'Don't worry! You still have me.'

"I never told her how disappointed I was not to be an official 'orphan.' Now, 40 years later, she's gone, too (she died a few years ago), and I really am an orphan, if an adult can be one. I haven't become a princess yet. But I sure miss Mom—and my dad, too."

Distant love: From **Shannon** of White Bear Lake:

"I'm calling to tell who I've never met but passionately love all the same. I thought and thought and thought about someone famous that everyone knew; that way, everyone would read it and understand. But I decided that there are two people that I passionately love without ever meeting them—and that's my biological parents. I was adopted, and I passionately love them because they loved me enough to give me up to a family that . . . I couldn't ask for more; they're the best family anyone could ever have."

Sweet release: From **Princess Grace** of Mahtomedi:

"Lately, I've been feeling that my children are growing up so quickly, they don't need me as much. Well, my almost-8-year-old son just came into our room, right after being tucked into bed, and said: 'Mom, I just get so busy during the day, with school and playing, and all the love just builds up and up until I just have to hug and love you so much.'

"What a wonderful way to end the day: letting the love out."

Faint praise: Still more from Corn Dog Corner:

Kate of "a little chunk of God's country, over here in Wisconsin": "I used to make weekly visits to my husband's grandma, who's now passed on to a better world. As I would do things for her, she'd squint at me through her bifocals and smile fondly at me—and one day said: 'Boy, you know, Katie, my dear? You're a lot prettier than you used to be.' I think that was a compliment.

"Because I did favors for her all the time, she always wished she could do something in return. She always said she had very little money, so she couldn't leave me that—but she prayed that I would have a happy death. Can't beat that, can you?"

Deb of St. Paul: "When my son was 2, we were bathing together when he looked at me and said: 'Mommy, you've got a bunch of tummies.'

'Thanks to you, kid,' I said."

Grandma D. of St. Paul: "I was visiting my great-granddaughter, who's 4 years old, a few weeks ago. She put her hand on my cheek and patted me, and she said: 'Oh, Grandma, you're so pretty. You're just beautiful!'

"I said: 'Sweetheart, that's so nice! Thank you.'

"And she said: 'Now, if we could only do something about those wrinkles.' "

Jill of Inver Grove Heights: "The other morning, I was sitting there with my 6-year-old daughter, Michelle, and we were looking out the window. I touched her face, and I said: 'Your skin is so soft and beautiful. I wish I had it.' She looked at mine—that day, I happened to have makeup on; I don't, normally—and she said: 'I like yours—'cause it looks like plastic. It feels like wax. And I like the holes you have in it, and the hair that's on it. I like yours because it feels like your pillowcase, Mom. I'd trade you any day.' "

Jennifer of Mounds View: "It's Thanksgiving, and my grandpa looks at me and says: 'Jen, you look real pretty today.'

"I said: 'Thanks, Grandpa.'

"And he says: 'Your skin looks so nice and fresh.'

"And I said: 'Thanks, Grandpa. I have makeup on today.'

"He said: 'No, that's not it. You don't have as many zits as you usually do.'

"Thanks, Gramps."

Pat of Arden Hills: "A couple nights ago, I was helping my 6-year-old son brush his teeth, and after he was done, I told him they looked all sparkly and white—and he told me that he'd rather have them look golden, like mine.

"I guess it's time to cut back on the coffee."

Mothers and sons: A call on the day before Mother's Day, from **Tanya** of Little Canada, speaking in a totally charming Dixie drawl:

"We're sittin' here today with absolutely nothing to do. Our road's under construction, and the guys didn't put enough gravel down, so my car's stuck out in the mud. I was just sittin' in here, watchin' TV; my 14-year-old got bored and went outside; I thought he was mowing the lawn.

"Well, he just came back in. He said: 'Look, Mom! You've gotta come look out the window!' I did—and he'd mowed, in the lawn, 'I LOVE YOU, MOM.' I thought that was the neatest thing—and by dang it, somebody should know about it besides me."

Best friends: From **B.J.B.** of the West Side:

"Several years ago, I was riding in the car with my 23-year-old stepdaughter, and she was sad and distraught and crying about a boyfriend who'd dumped her, and she bemoaned the fact that she had lost him and that she had no close girlfriends to commiserate with her—except for me, her stepmom.

"She said: 'You know, you're pretty much my best friend.' And then, after a short pause, she said: 'That's pretty pathetic, isn't it?'

"And then we both burst out laughing."

New tricks: From **Cindy** of Hudson, Wis.:

"My brother recently moved back home, at age 28. My parents have gotten real rigid in their schedules.

"My dad came home for lunch one time, and he had his pretzels out, with a sandwich, and he went to go to the bathroom, and my brother ate some of his pretzels.

"Dad comes back, and he goes: 'You ate some of my pretzels, Mike.'

"Mike said: 'I only ate one.'

"And my dad said: 'No, you ate three.'

"Well, he counts his pretzels every day and has exactly 10. Comes home at exactly 12:12 in the afternoon."

New tricks (II): From **Sue** of Woodbury:

"My parents are in their 80s, and I went back to visit them one weekend. And my mom and I got up on a Sunday morning, and I asked her if we were planning on going to church, and if my dad was planning on going.

"She said: 'No. Not going.'

"I said: 'How did you know that? He's not even up yet.'

"She said: 'I went and looked at his feet.'

"I said: 'How could you tell from his feet?'

"And she said: 'When he takes a shower at night, before he goes to bed, he puts on the socks that he's planning to wear for the next day. If he has black socks on, he's going to go to church; if he has white socks on, he's going to put his blue jeans on and stay home.'

"I thought it was cute."

Season's greetings: From **Sheryl K.** of St. Paul:

"I'm a recovering alcoholic—one of the real lucky ones in life. My oldest son was 13 by the time I realized what it was I'd done with my life. I guess that I destroyed a lot of his life in the process of trying to figure out how to run my own—'cause the kid didn't have much faith in anything at the point when I quit drinking. Didn't believe in God, didn't believe in Santa Claus, and certainly didn't believe in me.

"The Christmas after I quit drinking, I really lamented over some of the things that I had done to him—and I wanted to turn it around. What I did was: I said some prayers, and in one of those wonderful, miraculous moments, my H.P. [BULLETIN BOARD CLARIFIES, for those who need clarification: Higher Power] answered 'em and gave me a divine disguise in which to fool my son, so to speak.

"I went to our basement and hid gifts all over, in places that he normally would walk, and I made some noise in the rafters—and left some gifts cleverly enough disguised that even I was kind of in awe of myself. When I was all done with it, I went upstairs, where he had been sitting—he had assumed I was out in the kitchen, cooking—and I said: 'You know, the noises in the basement are really bothering me, and I don't want to go down there alone. Would you come and check things out with me?'

"He did. He went down the stairs first, and there, lo and behold, were wrapped packages. And he turned around and looked at me, and the look in his eyes was the most incredible thing that I have ever seen—because it was in that exact moment that I knew he believed, with all his heart, in Santa Claus, in God, and in me, and it was in that exact moment that I knew, with all my heart, that I believed in Santa Claus, in God, and in me."

Growing up, moving on: From **Dan** of White Bear Lake:

"Shortly after I arrived home from work, my 19-year-old son asked me if I'd like to play catch. I said, 'Sure'—as I had on countless other occasions during his lifetime.

"After the first few tosses, the realization came to me that the two of us may not have too many more opportunities like this in the future. It was pretty tough locating and catching the next few tosses through very misty eyes."

And from **Over-60 Mom** of Somerset, Wis.:

"Last week, I enjoyed a perfect evening—attending *My Fair Lady* at the State Theater in Minneapolis. This perfect evening was made sweet by the wonderful music; by seeing and hearing Richard Chamberlain, one of my longtime-favorite performers; and by the fact that my young and beautiful daughter took me. What a wonderful evening.

"But then, as the audience rose to give a standing ovation, the bitter kind of hit me as I realized that Richard Chamberlain, who is but a year or so younger than I, is now the elderly Professor Higgins, and that the stars who made the movie I so loved—Rex Harrison, Audrey Hepburn—are no longer with us.

"I now, like Richard Chamberlain, am in the senior bracket, and soon my daughter will be attending the theater with someone else. Our ways will part.

"As I applauded during the standing ovation, the tears streamed down my face. God, life is wonderful—made especially so that night by my beloved daughter.

"Thanks, Tootsie. Love you past the stars."

Race against time: From **Michelle** of Lake Elmo:

"The other night, I was sitting in the rocking chair, and my daughter, who is 7, cuddled up with me, put her head on my shoulder and let me rock her to sleep. It was such a bittersweet moment.

"She hasn't let me do that since she was a baby, and I thought it was so nice to be able to just sit there and cuddle with her and rock her to sleep— but on the other hand, it's probably the last time she'll ever let me do it.

"So to all you moms out there, with the little babies that are driving you nuts: Enjoy it, 'cause it goes by *so* fast."

Let Bygones be bygones: From **The Newcomer** of St. Paul:

"Beware! Highly sentimental thoughts ahead:

"Almost eight years ago, my only sibling, my older sister, died at age 30. Now, whenever I hear about siblings or other family members fighting a lot, or not speaking to each other for years, I want to throttle them for not appreciating what they have.

"Life shouldn't be about holding on to petty grudges and cutting people out of your life, because then you just end up bitter and alone. It should be about forgiveness and understanding, and increasing the love and fulfillment in your life."

Holding on, letting go: Look at your parents, you young people, and know this: Every one of them knows just how it feels for **Axman** of Mondovi, Wis.:

"When my daughter was 4 or 5, we were getting ready to cross the street one day, and she looked up and reminded me: 'Daddy, hold my hand so I won't die!'

"Today, at 15, she is edging toward young womanhood and no longer asks me to hold her hand when we cross the street. But even now, whenever I recall that scene, I think: 'Oh, my sweet little girl, if it were only that simple, how tightly and how steadily I would hold your hand!' "

CHAPTER 10

Warning!
Cute Kid Stories Ahead!

A torrent of wonderful stories about children began with this early-morning call from **Anonymous Mom** *of the northeast suburbs:*

"Last night, I was up working 'til midnight, and my husband was working 'til 1. I had the alarm set for 5:30 so I could get a bit more done before the kids got up this morning. About 4:15, the 3-year-old comes in, leans over to me and says: 'Mom, what can I do?' *[At this point, Anonymous Mom laughed a laugh of pure, joyful resignation.]* How do you answer something like that? *[And there's that laugh again—breathy and weary, but fully alive.]*

"The joys of parenting. Thanks."

Tom of the Midway: "Several years ago, we decided to take a vacation with my wife's parents and our daughter, who was about 3 at the time.

"One evening, we decided to go out to dinner. While the rest of us finished getting ready, our daughter went for a stroll with her grandpa. He was a kind man who had recently retired from the railroad. Unfortunately, some of his language was not left behind in the roundhouse. As we caught up with them, I remember it being such a picturesque sight: the two of them, side by side, next to a small pond, where two swans were swimming around.

"The silence was broken when from this little angel with frilly dress and patent-leather shoes came the words: 'Don't go near them, Dad. They're mean bastards.' "

A Happy Mom of Forest Lake: "Last week, my kids and my husband and I were driving down a road that goes through a low, swampy area. My 4-year-old son, Dillon, noticed the cattails and yelled out: 'Look! That's where they grow hot dogs!'

"Kids are the best entertainment ever."

Cy Cosgrove of Burnsville: "During the Christmas holidays, my granddaughter Mary Kate from Mystic, Connecticut, was visiting. Mary Kate is 3 years old, and while we were driving by the Black Dog power plant, high puffs of smoke were streaming out of the stack.

"Mary turned to me and asked: 'Poppy, is this where they make clouds?' "

Grandma Pat of White Bear Lake: "When our daughter Betsy was about 3 years old, she was saying good-bye to her grandma when Grandma looked down and said: 'Betsy, your shoes are on the wrong feet.'

"Betsy looked at her and said: 'But Grandma, these *are* my feet.' "

Muffy of Stillwater, reminiscing about her daughter's second day of kindergarten: "She looked up at me and said: 'Why are you crying, Mom?'

"I said: 'Oh, I'm just kinda sad, 'cause my baby's going to school.'

"And she said: 'Don't be sad. This is a whole new life for me.' "

Susan of Stillwater: "When my son was in kindergarten, we got this notice informing us that he would soon get his report card. Since it was his very first one, I explained to him how it worked (what an A was, and all the way to F).

"A few weeks later, over dinner, he blurted out: 'I got my report card yesterday'—and began to cry.

"Turns out his grades came inside a manila envelope (you pull the grade sheet out from the top), but he didn't know this. All he saw was the cover envelope with his name printed on it, and then, underneath, it said: 'Grade: K'—for kindergarten, but he didn't know this.

"He lay in bed all night thinking: 'A, B, C, D, E, F, G, H, I, J, K. Boy, did I do a *really* bad job.'

"Poor kid."

Grandma Carol of Mounds View: "My daughter Pat, living in Texas, is raising a family of animal-lovers. She has two dogs and a cat, so it's only natural for her 2½-year-old daughter, fearless Mary, to think all dogs are puppies, waiting to be played with.

"A stray dog had been hanging around their house for a couple of days, despite all attempts to discourage it, and Pat was determined that Mary, along with sister Carole, learn to stay away from strange animals. Mary was equally determined to play with it.

"Pat sat her down and said, firmly: 'Now Mary, you listen to me.' And Mary, with a serious expression to match Pat's, gave her mom undivided attention. 'That puppy doesn't live around here. You don't know that puppy, and that puppy doesn't know you.'

"Mary thought it over, went to the open door and loudly announced: 'Puppy, I'm Mary.'

"With social amenities satisfied, she went toward her new friend."

Shirley of Marine: "My friend Chet took his neighbors' 5-year-old daughter to the store with him, and when they came back out, he opened the car door for her. She asked him why he did that. He said he was being a gentleman. She said: 'What's that?' So he proceeded to explain to her what a gentleman was.

"When they got home, she remained in her seat. She said: 'You can open the door for me now.' Cute."

Marge of Little Canada: "My granddaughter Danielle and I went out to lunch one day when she was about 6. It was a really nice restaurant, and I told her she had to get dressed up.

"So we went into the restaurant, and she wanted a hamburger and french fries, and I told her she would have to order it herself—which she did. We got the hamburger and french fries, and the hamburger was quite large, so I leaned over and cut it in half.

"She looked at me with these big eyes and tears down her cheeks, and she says: 'Grandma! You broke it!' "

Lynn of St. Paul: "Yesterday morning, I was watching my 5-year-old daughter get dressed. She was struggling to make very tight underwear feel OK.

"So I said: 'Gee, honey, those undies are really getting tight on you. I'll have to pack 'em in the box for the poor people.'

"She turned and just stared at me and said: 'But Mom, why do the poor people want to wear tight underwear?' "

Betsy of Roseville: "When our son was about 3 years old, I think, we used to walk over to his grandparents' quite often, and he *always* would ask for something. This time, I said to him: 'Now, don't ask Grandma for *anything*. Understand?' Yes.

"So we got over there, and everything was fine—for just a little while. And then he went over to Grandma, put his hand on her knee and said: 'Grandma, what have you got that I'm not supposed to ask for?' "

Kathy of St. Paul: "Several years ago, when my daughter was about 2½, we were shopping for cards in a card shop, and a big guy with a black-leather jacket and chains and tattoos up and down his arms and legs came into the store.

"My daughter walked up to him, pulled on his vest, and said: 'You shouldn't color on your arms. You should color on paper.' "

Vicki's Friend of St. Cloud: "My friend had gone into the bathroom, and she was sitting on the toilet when my daughter walked in on her. And my daughter said: 'Wow! Your mommy lets you write on you?'

"She was looking at my friend's varicose veins."

J.J. of River Falls, Wis.: "It was a very hot summer. Our oldest son, Randy, then 4, was watching his mother nurse his baby brother. At each meal, Mother had two very large glasses at her place—one filled with milk and the other with cold iced tea. Randy, carefully analyzing the situation, asked: 'Which one is the iced-tea nipple, Mommie?' "

Peggy of Marine on St. Croix: "When my son was about 3 years old, we went and visited my parents in southern Wisconsin. And in the course of the week that we spent there, my mother's 12-year-old cat got very, very ill, and we were running back and forth to the vet quite often. While we were there, she had to make the difficult decision to put the cat to sleep.

"A few days after we got home, my son wanted to call up Grandma and see how she was doing, 'cause he knew she was really upset. So we called her up, and she gets on the phone, and he says—in this sweet, very concerned little voice that only a small child can have: 'Hi, Grandma. How's your dead cat doing?' Just one of those moments."

Carol of Houlton, Wis.: "Approximately 21 years ago, when one of our three sons was about 2½ years old, I was busy planting iris bulbs in our front yard. As you may know, they are really ugly, misshapen-looking bulbs. After watching me for a moment, my son asked me: 'What are you doing?' And I replied: 'I'm planting this'—holding up the bulb—'and next spring, a beautiful flower will come up.'

"With a look of amazement on his face, he said: 'What are they now—poop?' "

Chris of Falcon Heights: "When I was pregnant with my second child, my first child was about 3 years old, and he asked how that baby got in there. I tried to explain it in nice, easy terms, and he still didn't get it. He said: 'No, how'd that baby get in there?' I said: 'Well, remember when we planted the garden, and we put seeds in the ground, and carrots grew?' And he said: 'Yeah.' And I said: 'Well, it's the same thing. Dad planted the seed in Mom, and a baby's growing.' And he was real quiet, and he said: 'How'd you get all that dirt in there?' "

Roni of St. Paul: 'One day, me, my sister and her daughter Becky were sitting around the table talking about where babies come from. Becky's 3½ years old. Emily told Becky that she came out of her tummy. Becky sat there, with a real serious look on her face, and then she looked at her mother and said: 'Why did you eat me?' "

Berdella of Roseville: "I heard my brother ask his little grandson: 'What do you want to be when you grow up?' The little boy answered: 'I want to be retired.' "

Renell of Bloomington: "I was in a store in Bloomington with a friend of mine, and a gentleman had his little son with him; he was about, oh, 4 or 5, and he was kinda blocking the aisle when we tried to pass. I said: 'Excuse me.' And this father looked down at his little son and said: 'Say "Excuse me," son.'

"The little boy looks up, and he goes: 'Excuse me.' Then he looks up at his dad with great big innocent eyes, so apologetic, and says: 'Daddy, did I [expel a posterior breeze]?'

"It was *so* cute. Everybody that heard it started laughing."

Susan D. of St. Paul: "I have a gem of wisdom from my daughter, when she was 5 years old. On the drive through the country to my mother's house, there was a beautiful evergreen tree growing in front of a farm. I called it 'my favorite tree' and looked forward to appreciating it each time I made the trip. But a couple of years ago, during a drive to Grandma's, I was dismayed to see that the tree had been cut down. My 5-year-old daughter, Laura, was more positive about the situation. She said: 'Now it'll just have to be your favorite stump, Mom.' "

Joni of North St. Paul: "My granddaughter is 9 years old. We went to the cemetery to visit my husband's grave and my mother's grave; they're quite close together. We visited with my husband, Bob, and then walked over and noticed—I hadn't been there since the snow left—that next to my mother was a new person. And I said: 'Shannon, look! Great-grandma has a new neighbor.' She looked at me, put her hand on her head, and said: 'Well, Grandma, he's probably dead.' "

Gary of Stillwater: "When my little boy was 2 years old—his name is Jevan— I was in the backyard digging some holes to install a swing set. I was out there with the post-hole digger, and he was out there at the same time, play- ing with a toad that he found back there. He eventually got bored and walked away, to the other end of the yard.

"Time passed, and eventually, as I was diggin' the hole for the post, I hit a rock; I reached down into the hole to grab the rock, which was about the size of my fist, and I pulled it out of the hole, and as hard as I could, I threw it down into the woods. As I was throwing this rock, I looked down to the other end of the house, and I saw Jevan—and he had this look on his face, like ab- solute horror.

"He looked down into the woods, and with this sad, grieving look on his face, and in a sad, grieving tone of voice, he said: 'Bye, toad.' "

Karl of St. Cloud: "My sister came up to St. Cloud last weekend with her 2½-year-old daughter. They passed a field with some horses in it, and my sis- ter pointed 'em out to her daughter and said: 'Look! There's some horses!'

"And my niece goes: 'Holy cow!'

"My sister just looked at her and said: 'Where did you hear that?'

"My niece just says: 'From my mouth.' "

Deanna Olson of New Brighton: "I have a 2½-year-old daughter named Ashley. One day, she was on the couch, and she was saying: 'Damn! Damn! Damn!'

"I went out there, and I said: 'Ashley, are you saying "Damn!"?'

"She said: 'Yeah.'

"And I said: 'You can't say that. That's a naughty word. If you want to say something, you can say: 'Holy cow!'

"She said: 'Oh! OK!'

"The next time I go into the living room, she looks up at me and says: 'Damn cow.' "

Ed of Woodbury: "Matthew, 8, and Alicia, 5, were watching their mother, my daughter, change diapers on Emily Rose, 8 months, when Matthew picked up the baby thermometer from the changing table—in its case, fortunately—and stuck it in his mouth.

" 'Take it out of your mouth,' his mother ordered. 'That's a rectal thermometer.'

" 'What's that, Mom?' he asked.

"His little sister explained, 'It's for when your butt's sick.' "

Grandma Emily of St. Paul: "Last night, my grandson was visiting, and he wanted to play Trivial Pursuit. Just having turned 5, he's too young to answer the questions that come with the game, so we make them up.

"I asked him what had four legs and a back, but could not move or walk. He started to name some animals, so I gave him the clues again. I had in mind: a chair. He shouted excitedly, as only a 5-year-old can: 'A *dead* horse!' "

Mergatroid of St. Paul: "We had a guest for dinner awhile ago, and he inadvertently passed gas, quite audibly, at the dinner table. My husband and I politely ignored it, hoping to spare his dignity, but our 3-year-old looked right at him and cheerfully said: 'God bless you.' "

Bev of Woodbury: "My granddaughter Holly, when she was about 4, was saying her prayers one night, and she said to her mother: 'What does God look like?'

"Her mother thought for a minute, and she said: 'Well, I don't really know. What do you think God looks like?'

"Holly thought for a while, and then she said: 'I think he looks like Pat Sajak.' "

Mel of Minnetonka: "I was just sending my 3-year-old to bed, and he said he didn't feel good. I said: 'Well, what hurts?' And he said: 'My feelings.' "

Elsie of St. Paul: "Our 4-year-old granddaughter is into numbers. She said: 'Grandpa, I know how old my mother is.' He said: 'How old is that?' She said: '33 years old. How old are you, Grandpa?' He said: '71.' She said: 'Did you start with 1?' "

Dewey of La Crosse, Wis.: "The other day while baby-sitting my friend's 2-year-old boy, Zachary, I was talking to him close-up when he said to me, 'Your mouth has a smelly wind in it.' "

Larry Werner of Hastings: "I have false teeth—and one day when my granddaughter Missy was about 3 years old, I was driving down the road and I had a little seed under my lower plate. I took it out of my mouth—and Missy saw me take 'em out; she didn't know Grandpa had false teeth.

"She said: '*Gimme* them!'—and she made a grab for 'em—'They're *Grandma's!*' "

The Trophy Wife of St. Paul: "I picked up my son and another little boy from school yesterday.

"My son looked at the little boy and said: 'You know, my daddy worked *all . . . night . . . long* last night. He didn't even come home.'

"The other little boy said: 'Well, my uncle and my grandmother and my grandfather—they do that all the time.'

"My son said: 'Well, I've got a grandfather who can pull his teeth out of his mouth and put it in water!'

"And the other little kid just looked at him, like: 'Oh, boy. Can't beat *that*.' "

Randy of South St. Paul: "My little boy, who was 4, had a habit of getting up in the middle of the night to use the bathroom. While I was in the bathroom remodeling, I had pulled the toilet out so I could walk around a little bit better. I set it in his bedroom—not thinking that he would get up at 12 o'clock at night to use the bathroom. I was in the bathroom, finishing up the job, and I heard some banging around in his bedroom. I went in and opened up the door, and here's my boy sitting on the toilet. I said: 'Brandon, what are you doing?' He says: 'I'm goin' to the bathroom!' I said: 'No, you're not!'—in half disbelief. Then he stood up and said: 'Yeah, I am. Look!' "

Louise of St. Paul: "My husband and I were visiting some friends who have a 2-year-old who's quite precocious. In the morning, when he was shaving in the bathroom, my husband happened to look down and see that he had not quite closed the door. He sees this little 2-year-old's eyes through about a three-inch space.

"She looked up at him and said: 'Hi! Do you want the door closed?'

"He said: 'Well, yes! Thanks!'

"So she stepped inside and closed the door."

Matt of St. Paul: "When I was in the Army, in 1977, I'd just been made a sergeant. I decided to come home in uniform to show off to my 2-year-old daughter and my wife and my brand-new son.

"My son had been born a couple months previously—and my daughter was very curious as to why he had . . . an extra little thing . . . and my wife gave her the proper name for it. She said: 'Is Daddy a boy, too?' And my wife said: 'Yes, Daddy's a boy, too.' She said: 'Daddy's got one of those?' 'Yeah, yeah.'

"So I came home; I got off the plane, and my wife and my daughter were there to greet me. My daughter was in a little blue dress, and she was just delighted as I came up the ramp. She said: 'Daddy! Daddy!'—and I was in my uniform, and I felt really great; you know, here's this cute little girl saying 'Daddy! Daddy!' to me.

"I said: 'Elizabeth!'

"She said: 'Daddy, you bring your penis with you?' "

Barb of the East Side: "Our daughter was teaching her 3½-year-old son that he should never let anyone touch his private parts. One day, he was in the bathroom and she opened the door to check on him. He said: 'Don't come in. I don't want you to see my favorite parts.'

"We decided he's a typical male."

A.C. of White Bear Lake: "My sister and her husband live in a place called Beatty, Nevada. It's about 75 miles or so outside of Las Vegas. One time, they were traveling back to Beatty from a day in Las Vegas, where they do most of their shopping, with their son, my nephew, who was about 4 or 5 years old at the time.

"David was in the back, and at one point during the trip, he had to go to the bathroom—and he let them know that. They said: 'Hang on just a little bit, David, 'cause we'll be home soon.' He was quiet for a little bit—but after a while, he let them know again that he had to go to the bathroom. They said: 'We're gonna be home pretty soon, David. Just hold on a little bit longer. Just a little bit longer.'

"Finally, from the backseat, David says: 'Mommy, Mommy! My penis is going without me!' "

Peggy of St. Paul: "I was driving down the street, and my 2-year-old niece Kayla was in the backseat holding her Ernie doll.

"She says: 'I have to go potty!'

"I turned and said: 'Honey, can you hold it for a few minutes?'

"Her answer: 'No, I'm holding Ernie!' "

Judy of Woodbury: "My sister was riding along with her grandchild, who's probably about 3 or 4, and as she was riding along, she was thinking about what she referred to her parents as—which was 'Mother' and 'Daddy.' And she was wondering what her own daughter called her, so she turned to her granddaughter and asked her: 'What does your mom call *me*?" And her granddaughter looked up and said: 'Nut case.' "

Mary Helen's Sister of Coon Rapids: "When my sister was 7 or 8 years old, my parents were having a dinner party. My parents and their friends were sitting around the dining-room table, having coffee, when my sister Mary stomped into the dining room wearing no clothes at all, angrily put her hands on her hips and stated: 'No one is giving me . . . any . . . privacy!' "

Margaret of Minneapolis: "My husband and I just returned from visiting my sister and her husband in Washington State. Our first night there, my sister made this big meal—and afterwards, I was upstairs changing, with my 4-year-old niece, Molly, watching the whole process with great interest. I said: 'That was a great meal. Your mom sure is a good cook—but I'm really full.' Molly said: 'Yes. I noticed that your bottom's a little bit fat.' "

Ellen of Minneapolis: "When my daughter, Katherine, was 3 years old, she was looking at my long, beautiful, gorgeous fingernails, and she said, 'Mama, when I get big, can I have fingernails like yours?'

"And I said, 'Oh, I'm sure you will.'

"Then she said, 'But could I have prettier hair?' "

Jan of Cottage Grove: "My 3-year-old granddaughter, Molly, is the funniest child I know. The other day, she was scratching in her ear. When she finished, she looked at her finger and saw a little blob of earwax on it. She said: 'Who put a booger in my ear?' "

Another **Jan** of Cottage Grove: "About two months ago, my 5-year-old son, Sam, was sitting on the couch when I walked into the room. He said: 'Hey, Mom! You know that stuff that comes out of your ear?' I said: 'Yeah.' And he said: 'It doesn't taste good.' "

Vicki of Maplewood: "Last week, I was watching TV, and my 3½-year-old son Jerry was doing the same in the chair. I looked over at him and caught him digging for gold (picking his nose). I told him not to do that.

"Five minutes later, I caught him again. I told him one more time not to do that.

"Jerry looked me straight in the eye and said: 'I know, Mom. I'm putting it back!' "

Vicki of St. Paul: "When my niece was about 4 years old, she was in a restaurant with my brother and his wife. They don't allow their children to chew gum, and she was just sitting there at the table chewing gum. And her mother turns to her and goes: 'Becky, where'd you get that gum from? Spit it out!'

"And she looks underneath the table, points, and she goes: 'There, Mom! There's lots of it! Do you want some?' "

Kim of Woodbury: "My young children are still working on their Halloween buckets, and this evening my 5-year-old son asked me if I wanted some peanuts—holding out a handful of nuts. I said: 'No, thanks. Where did you get them?'—thinking he must have found a pushed-aside gift package from last Christmas. His reply: 'I hatched them from my M&Ms.' Glad I said no."

Barb Walsh of Lake Elmo: "My daughter, Abby, when she was 2, had a real caterpillar fixation. She wouldn't go anywhere unless she had a caterpillar in her hand. One day, I noticed that her hands were empty, and I said: 'Abby, where's your caterpillar?' She made a noise that can't be spelled—something like *mmmm-bulggh*—and she spit a caterpillar out of her mouth into her hand! She'd just decided that was a good place to carry it."

Laurie of St. Croix Falls, Wis.: "A friend of ours went deer hunting last year, shot a huge buck and had the head mounted. It's hanging on a wall in his basement. My son went and saw it one night, and he kept looking around on the other side of the wall. Finally went up to the guy and said: 'You shoot the *butt* off that deer?' "

Deb of Oakdale: "I was sick for a few days in a row, and not getting much done around the house, and I told my 8-year-old daughter, Jesse, how I felt kind of worthless.

"She looked at me very sympathetically and patted me on the knee and said: 'You *are* worthless, Mom.' "

The Girls' Mom of Mendota Heights: "When I frown or squint, I get two vertical lines between my eyes. OK, they're wrinkles. A few years back, when my daughter was 3, I was talking to her rather seriously about how to treat her new sister—and I was pleased because she seemed to be paying such close attention to me. When I finished, I asked if she had any questions, and she said: 'Yes. Why is there an 11 between your eyes?' "

Peggy of Shoreview: "I'm blessed with children—ages 2, 4, 5 and 7—who sleep later than most kids I know of, and because of that, their father has usually left for work or wherever he needs to go before they've gotten up. On Valentine's morning, I had just awakened, about 8:30, and I was sitting up in bed, and in walked my 4-year-old. He pointed to the person next to me in bed—his father, by the way—and said: 'Who's *that*?' "

Cindy of Cottage Grove: "Years ago, we had house guests. Their child's name was Dell, and Dell was pretty high-strung; his mom was trying very hard to keep him behaving. Dell was about 3 or 4, I guess, and running around the house, blowing a whistle.

"She said: 'Dell, Dell, Dell! We don't blow the whistle in the house!'

"And he said: 'Oh, OK.'

"The next thing we knew, he was outside, and we were listening to the noise coming in through the windows: whistling, whistling, whistling. And she said: 'Dell, Dell, Dell!'

" 'What, Mama?'

" 'We don't blow the whistle outside!'

"He came up to her and looked her straight in the face—and very seriously, with a need-to-know look on his face, he said: 'Mama, where do we blow the whistle?' "

Shari of Fridley: "My 4-year-old daughter and my 2-year-old son and I were on the way to the bookstore. When I told my daughter where we were going, she asked if it was the one with the water fountain by it. I told her it was, and she said that while I was in the bookstore, she was gonna go look at the water fountain. I told her she couldn't, that she had to stay with Mom and that afterwards we would go look at the water fountain.

"She told me that she'd be a good girl—and to *please* let her go look at the water fountain. I figured it was time for one of those mother-daughter talks where you tell 'em about the bad people in the world. So I told her that there's people out there who don't have pretty little girls and boys, and when they see them all by themselves, sometimes they take them home with them and won't let them see their mommies and daddies again.

"She understood and said, 'OK, Mom, I'll stay with you while you're in the bookstore.'

"I figured: 'OK. One strike for Mom; I did good this time.'

"She was quiet for a few minutes, and then I hear her calling me: 'Mom?'

"And I go: 'Yeah?'

"And she goes: 'Where'd you and Daddy find me and Brett?'

"I didn't know what to say."

Ruth of Brooklyn Center: "My husband, my 4-year-old granddaughter and I were at our cabin up north, looking out the window, eating dinner—and a big woodchuck came by our car. It proceeded to crawl into the motor; my husband opened the hood, and we tried to poke him out, but he wouldn't move. We were afraid he'd chew off the wires, or whatever.

"So my husband went to the cabin and got his gun. He said: 'If he ever comes out, I'm gonna shoot him.' Shortly afterward, the woodchuck came out, and my granddaughter was standing in the window, looking, and my husband shoots it. My granddaughter had never seen anything like that; she was a city kid.

"My husband then buried him—dug a hole, put the woodchuck in it, and stomped it down, packed the dirt over the woodchuck.

"That evening, we went to the cemetery to put flowers on my husband's folks' grave. My granddaughter said: 'Who's buried here?' And my husband said: 'Well, it's my mother and dad.'

"She looked up at us and said: 'Did you shoot *them*, too?' "

G.G. of St. Paul: "My 5-year-old grandson, Bobby, was mourning the death of 16-year-old Reuben, the family dog. I felt very sorry for him one day when his playmates were discussing their pet poodle and dachshund. But Bobby announced, very proudly, with a smile: 'Well, *we* have a *dead* dog.' "

Bill of Maplewood: "My 3½-year-old daughter was looking through a catalog and saw a picture of a cat on a rug and said: 'Boy, I sure wish we could get a cat, Daddy.'

"I said: 'Yeah, I know, but you know Daddy's allergic.'

"She says: 'Yeah, I know.' She paused, and then she brightened and said: 'But we could always get one when you die!' "

Grandma Terrie of Columbia Heights: "My almost-3-year-old grandson, Anthony, has been living with me for most of his life, while his mom is getting her life in order.

"One morning, a county social worker was visiting with us at our home. When she asked me how I was doing (grand)parenting again, I told her: 'Most days with Anthony are wonderful; he's a joy and a treat to be with. But there are those days when it's a pain.'

"Without missing a beat, Anthony said: 'In the a—, Grandma?' "

BULLETIN BOARD MUSES: We bet that social worker was impressed.

JB's Wife: "One day when my youngest son, Ben, was almost 3, we were spending the day at my mom's house. It was time for Ben to take his nap, and Gramma T. told him to go pick out *one book*, and she would read it to him before he had to lie down. The next thing we know, Ben walked into the room struggling to carry the biggest book he could find—the *Physician's Desk Reference*. We don't know how he managed to pull it down from the top shelf of the bookcase.

"Same kid, same Gramma, a few years later. Ben came into the living room and proudly announced that he had stepped on the scale, and one of his legs weighed 36 pounds. Gramma told him to go weigh his butt, so he sat on the scale and couldn't believe that his butt weighed that much.

"Then Gramma's mean streak came out, and she told him to go weigh his head. The rest of us all started laughing, but good old Ben gave it a try. A few minutes later, he came out to tell Gramma that he'd tried and tried, but no matter how he weighed his head, he couldn't read the numbers on the scale."

Mary of Mahtomedi: "In preschool this week, they're doing color mixing—you know, the old 'two drops of red and two drops of yellow, and you get orange'—all that cool stuff.

"Well, I was cleanin' the toilet out and put in all that blue stuff to make it look good, and my 4-year-old walked into the room and brightly said: 'You know, Mom, if I pee in there, we can make green!'

"I just want to publicly thank his teacher for passing on that life skill to my little guy."

Kris of Woodbury: "Two years ago, I worked with a toddler teacher at a day-care center. A 3-year-old girl came into the room to visit her little brother. A little toddler was crying, so the 3-year-old went over to her and said in a sweet voice: 'It's OK.' The toddler continued crying, so the 3-year-old put her hands on her hips, stomped her foot and told her: 'I . . . *said* . . . it's . . . OK!' "

Foxy Roxy of St. Paul: "Yesterday, the kids were suffering from cabin fever from being inside, 'cause it was so cold. My 6-year-old, Becky, just didn't know what to do, and I said: 'Well, why don't you sit down at the computer and write a story.' And she wrote this lovely story:

" 'YOU ARE MY MOM AND YOU ARE MY DAD AND I LOVE YOU MOM AND I LOVE YOU TO DAD AND I LOVE YOU JESSICA AND I LOVE YOU TO CHRIS AND I LOVE YOU TO SMOKEY AND I LOVE MY TOYS AND I LIKE READ MY BOOK AND I LIKE PLAYING WITH MY FRIENDS AND I LIKE COLORING PICTURES AND I LIKE DOING MATH AND I LIKE PLAYING WITH LEGOS AND I LIKE SCHOOL AND I LIKET SEEING MRS. DOUBTFIRE. THET'S MY BOOK OF I LOVE EVERYBODY AND I LIKE EVERYBODY. BY BECKY.'

"It was really cute: While she was doing it, I was upstairs working in the bedroom (we're remodeling), and she'd run upstairs and say: 'Mom, how do you spell "coloring"?' So I'd spell it slowly for her: C-O-L-O-R-I-N-G. She'd run back downstairs. Pretty soon, there's the footsteps coming back upstairs again, and she'd say: 'Mom, what comes after the C?'

"Took her a little while to write this. Most of the words, she spelled by herself; the only ones she asked about were 'coloring,' 'playing' and 'Doubtfire.'

"I tell ya: That little story really made my day. I wish everybody could like everybody, too."

Grandma Bonnie of St. Paul: "A couple of weeks ago, when my littlest granddaughter, Maggie, was over, we were going to give the puppy a bath—and didn't have any puppy shampoo. I used cat shampoo. Maggie was really concerned. She put her little hands on each side of the little puppy's face and said: 'Don't worry, Benjamin. When it's all over, you'll still be a dog.'"

Linda of Woodbury: "The other day, I was driving in the car with my 2½-year-old daughter, and I drove across an intersection at McKnight and 36 a little faster than usual in order to make a green light—and with the dip in the road there, it gave the car kind of a roller-coaster effect.

"My daughter looked at me and kind of giggled, and I said: 'Was that fun? Did it tickle your tummy?'

"And she said: 'No, Mommy, it tickled my 'gina.' I laughed half the way home.

"When I told my brothers and sisters and my mom and dad about it at Christmas, they were all laughing hysterically, too—and then my mom asked: '*What* street was that?'"

Sharon M. of Lake Elmo: "My 4-year-old granddaughter had begun to talk about death. Sadly realizing that one day I would die, she said: 'Grandma, when I get old like you, I'm going to die, too. But you better wait, so we can do it together.'

"I'm going to give it my best shot."

CHAPTER 11

Joybubbles Time

*J*oybubbles of Minneapolis (legal name: Joybubbles) is one of a kind—a man who, at middle age, resolved to experience childhood. His had been stolen from him. Since that day in the spring of 1988, he has been 5 years old—and shall be until the day he dies. We called him "irrepressibly cheerful," until we learned better.

Everything about Joybubbles sets him apart, but nothing reveals his remarkableness more clearly than the stories he tells—both to the children's play groups that he entertains (he'd say: plays with) and to the readers of Bulletin Board.

Joybubbles is blind, you see, but you'd never, ever guess it. Listen:

During a discussion of product names:

"I read the comments about Joy dish soap being inappropriately named. Well, for me, it's brought a lot of joy.

"Naturally, I use it for play. Kids, when we get together, sit on the floor, with a great big old pan of it, sloshing it around to make bubbles, and pouring it into little cups and bigger cups, and squishing sponges.

"But there's one Joy dish-soap story that I cherish. Back in late 1989, a mommy invited me over to play every week with her little girl, who hadn't talked in about two years—ever since she had seen her father get shot and killed in Oklahoma. And even though I can't see and the little girl couldn't talk, somehow we just communicated and had a special relationship.

"One day, we were playing on the floor. We had just gotten finished rustling a big bunch of paper bags—which makes a wonderful sound. Anyway, we were playing with a pan of Joy dish soap when the little girl put her arms around my neck and hugged me—bubbles were dripping all down me—and I heard her whisper: 'Bubba-bubbles.' And then louder: 'Bubba-bubbles! Bubba-bubbles!'—about five or six more times. And the mommy and everybody, we were hugging and crying and laughing. It's one of those special times.

91

"Joy does make wonderful bubbles.

"During lunch, the little girl said 'Mommy!' really loud (and over the next few weeks, she talked more and more). When I was telling the mother what a privilege it was that she let me come play, and how it was a miracle that I just happened to be there on the day that the little girl would start talking, the mother said: 'You just name what you'd like, and I'll see that I get it for you.'

"I said: 'What I'd really most like is the bottle of Joy dish soap we used this morning.'

"I still have it. That was Monday, December 11, 1989, and after all those years, that Joy dish soap still makes wonderful bubbles. Sometimes, when I'm feeling sad and remembering bad childhood memories and stuff, I get that bottle out and play in those bubbles. It's nice to know that I have bubble friends for life.

"I don't think there's anything quite as wonderful as play.

"And just remember: Joy makes wonderful bubbles."

During a discussion of children's imaginary playmates that coincided with Mother's Day:

"One day when I was at the play group, I was talking about my imaginary friend that I regularly play with, named Emily Friend. And a little 4-year-old girl there was so excited that I had an imaginary friend that she told me about hers. She said: 'Mommy, let's tell Joybubbles about Bumpo!'

"She hopped in her mother's lap and told me about a day just shortly after she was adopted: She and her mother were driving towards some parenting meeting, and they had to take a potty-break stop, and then they drove and drove and drove, when all of a sudden she started crying just as hard as a little 4-year-old can cry, saying 'Oh, Mrs.! Mrs.! We left Bumpo!' She didn't call her new mommy 'Mommy,' because she'd say 'You're not my mommy. You're Mrs.'

"So she was crying really hard, and her mother said, 'Where did we leave him?'

"And she said: 'Way back at the potty!'

" 'Well, do you think he's still there?'

" 'Well, yeah, that's where we left him!'

" 'I could drive back there, and we could see if we could find him.'

"She said, 'Oh, that's too *far!*'

"But her mother said, 'Not for *me* it isn't.'

"So they drove back, and when they got there, the little girl jumped out of the car and found Bumpo—nobody else could see him—and brought him back to the car and was crying for joy and hugging him. She was bouncing up and down; I think if her seat belt wasn't fastened, she would have gone through the roof. And then she reached up and hugged her mother and said, 'Oh, Mommy! You found Bumpo! Oh, Mommy! You're my real mommy now. My other mommy would have never found Bumpo! Oh, Mommy!'

"And you know when you've adopted a little girl and you get to hear her call you Mommy for the very first time, that's truly one of the greatest Mother's Day gifts in the world.

"Well, I wish you tonight the motto of our play group, which is: We go apart to dream; we come together to play. I hope you have time for both.

"Good night, and Happy Mother's Day."

After Bulletin Board requested "Words from the wise":

"This is Joybubbles. My words of wisdom are: It's not your fault; you did the best you could at the time. I particularly address this to survivors of childhood sexual abuse, like me.

"Too often, we judge ourselves by who we are now and what we know now and what we do now. But we have to remember who we were then: a child, vulnerable, thinking that those grown-ups were there to take care of us and that we could trust them.

"Mine was in a Catholic school for the blind in New Jersey in 1955—by a nun, repeatedly. The physical abuse by a number of other nuns on me and my sister—we remembered that. But I never knew that I could forget something for so long—something that hurt so bad that I could forget for so long. I started to remember in April of '91.

"We judge ourselves by what we do now. They told me then that if I told my parents how bad I was in that school, my parents wouldn't want me. And I asked what that would mean, and they said: 'Well, I guess you'd go to a foster home or an orphanage.' And sometimes when Daddy'd be taking me out for ice cream or something, I was wondering if that was gonna be the foster home; maybe they had found out.

"They also told me a lot that God was watching me. Well, since I've been doing a lot of work on this, I've added one word to that—and it makes a lot of difference: God is watching *over* me. That one added word means a lot.

"I guess I want to say that sometimes when you're really hurting and these memories are awakened, you feel like you're coming apart—but that's just when you're beginning to come together, because when something's been numb for so long, it's bound to hurt when it awakens.

"You are a survivor. You can make it. Keep on with it. And remember: It's not your fault; you did the best you could at the time."

93

When Barney-bashing was all over the news:

"Barney, on TV, is really two people. Bob West is hidden away deep in a control room, doing the voice. And David Joyner wears the costume and does all of the movements. They coordinate it with a two-way radio link. Likewise for the other dinosaurs, Baby Bop and B.J.; they each have a voice person and a costume person.

"Wouldn't that be an interesting radio link to listen in on?

"But that's not the *real* Barney. The real Barney is the one that kids have as a playmate and a friend when the TV is turned off.

"Like my friend Jason, for instance: He knew the real Barney. He died when he was 4½, last March, and he would talk to Barney regularly—especially when he was real scared or sad or angry. He talked to Barney a lot about dying, and Barney told Jason that Barney would take him to Playland—this wonderful place where he wouldn't be sick anymore, and he'd be able to jump on the beds and everything again.

"One night, his mommy heard Jason talking to Barney and knocked on the door and said: 'Sweetie, could I come in and talk to him a little while?' And Jason, sort of unbelieving, said: 'You? Talk to Barney?' And Mommy said: 'Well, you know mommies know a little magic, too, darling.'

"So she came in and sat on the bed and hugged Jason tight and said: 'Now Barney, this is the most wonderful little boy—a very, very special little boy—and I love him a lot. Now you promise me you're gonna take care of him real good. There's some important things I need to tell you: He likes his sandwiches cut slantwise; he doesn't eat 'em if they're cut straight across—well, except for sugar-bread sandwiches; they're to be folded in half, with a little butter and lots of sugar inside. And you'd better have strong beds there in Playland, because he likes to jump on the beds, and he's really good at it.'

"She told Barney a lot of other real important things that are vital in caring for a little boy.

"And man, you should've heard Jason bragging to his little friends about having a mommy who could talk to Barney. And a few weeks later, he went to Playland.

"Jason's mommy still calls me, and she likes it when I let her know what she already knows—that she is still, and forever will be, Jason's mommy.

"If there's a Barney Fan Club out there, I'd like to find out where it is and join it and be the biggest 5-year-old Barney fan there is—because I talk to him, and he talks to me regularly, and I'm proud to say that I love Barney.

"And to Jason, who I know is well and happy in Playland, jumping on beds and eating lots of sugar-bread sandwiches and doing all kinds of really neat things, forever and ever when I listen to Barney on TV or listen to my Barney tapes, you'll be there in spirit. I'll never forget you.

"Shimbaree, shimberah—which, in this case, might mean: Goodbye, hello!"

And now, **an anonymous mother:** "This is for Joybubbles—and if I can get through this without crying, I'll be eternally grateful.

"I have a 13-year-old son who's terminal, and I'm a long-standing Barney hater. It's always driven me nuts that my nieces and nephews listen to that.

"Now, I have a new respect for Barney. I forgot that when my son first became ill, he took his Ewok with him to the hospital—the little fellows from the *Star Wars* movies who were cute and cuddly. That little Ewok took every shot my son took, went to surgery every time he had to, went through all of the painful procedures—and it reminded me that everybody needs somebody to help them when things aren't going so well.

"This afternoon, when I sit down and *watch* Barney for the first time, I'm going to look at it in a whole new light."

CHAPTER 12

Accidents of Mirth

Unfortunate for them, but not for the rest of us:

Head Cheese the Cheesehead: "I was in New Zealand a few years ago, fly-fishing. Nice little trip.

"I was on the banks of the Mattoro River on the South Island. It was sort of a boring day on the stream; nothing much happening. So I sat down with my fly rod underneath my arm, holding the small wet fly in my hand and eating a banana.

"While I was sitting there eating the banana, a nice four-pound brown swam by me. I thought: 'Well, it's a good time to try to catch it'; after they swim by, it's a good time to let a fly fly in front of them and see what happens.

"So I switched hands with the banana and the fly rod and the fly, and finished eating the banana, and swallowed. Looked around for my fly—and couldn't find it. And I thought: I couldn't have done what I think I've done—which I'd done. The fly had gotten into the banana, and I had swallowed it.

"I pulled on the line for a little bit, and it wouldn't come out, so I cut the line off—about three feet out in front of my mouth—and tied the line, the three-pound nylon, to my shirt, and rode my bicycle into town. Went to see the doctor, and they finally found it on the X-rays about three-quarters of the way down my esophagus.

"So I got to be operated on in Kew Hospital in Southland—one of the southernmost hospitals in the world. That was sorta neat."

Day-care Mom of Shoreview: "Several years ago, when I taught Sunday school for the first time, I was teaching 4-year-olds. It was Christmastime, and we were going to be lighting the Advent candles in our little worship service.

"I was lighting the fourth Advent candle—and all of a sudden, I look at my finger and it's on fire! I had long fingernails, and they were painted with nail polish. My fingernail was on fire!

96

"I looked at it and didn't know what to do; I decided to just blow it out. So I blew it out.

"I turned around, and all of the children were just staring at me, and one of them said: 'Wow! Do that *again!*'"

Grace of Lake Elmo: "I was vacuuming under my son's bed, and I wasn't paying attention. He had been out hunting, and I picked up a .22 shell from under the bed in my vacuum, which was a Hoover, and the beater bar set the bullet off, which ricocheted into the floor, which was a cement floor, came back and shot me in the leg."

Wacie of Woodbury: "My dad was strictly a desk jockey in his final years at work, but apparently dreamed of other things. One night, we all heard him let out a blood-curdling yell. The lights went on, and all five or six of us kids who were still at home came running downstairs to my parents' bedroom.

"My father was moaning in agony while holding his foot. My mother was trying to stifle laughs.

"On the way to the hospital, my mom told us that Dad said he was dreaming he was a motorcycle policeman, and a large dog was chasing him. Since my dad was terrified of dogs, he was kicking at the dog. And since his side of their bed was close to the wall, he kicked the wall and broke his toe.

"The medical staff at the hospital were trying not to laugh as they set his toe, but many guffaws were heard.

"The next day when my dad went to work, he gave my mother strict instructions that if his secretary phoned her asking about his mishap (because he knew she would), Mom was not to tell her how it happened.

"So, of course, my mom told the secretary everything."

Mike the Bartender of St. Paul: "I was working my way through school as a diesel mechanic in North Carolina, and my place of employment was located next to a deaf/mute school. Every day at the same time, a very pretty deaf/mute girl walked across our parking lot, and I would stop what I was doing and watch her—thinking that I wished I could communicate in sign language, because it must have been lonely for her in this town that I perceived to be intolerant of people's imperfections.

"One day, my partner and I were finishing up on a tractor-trailer engine we had secured on an engine stand when my pretty friend came waltzing across the lot at the prescribed hour. I leaned against the engine to watch her at the same moment my partner decided to fire up the engine. My hand got sucked into the fuel-pump drive, and it mashed the heck out of it.

"After that, I figured if I ever learned sign language, I'd probably speak with a lisp.

"Also: I called in previously to tell about the time I was caught between my truck and a concrete truck in New Orleans. What I hadn't mentioned was that the chute on the concrete truck caught me at hip level and snapped off my coccyx bone.

"When they got me to the hospital, the doctor said: 'Contrary to popular opinion, I can't put your a— in a sling.' I thought that was kinda cute.

"Still today, the first thing I look for in different bars is the amount of padding on the bar stools."

Butch of St. Paul: "I had gotten dentures on the bottom; they pulled all my teeth, and the dentist told me I should sleep with my dentures in my mouth—not take 'em out for a time, so my gums would shape to 'em.

"The first night, I wake up in the morning, and I have this terrible, terrible pain in my hip. I had spit out my teeth, and I was lying on my teeth; they had imbedded into my hip.

"Makes me one of the only people in the world who can bite himself in the a—."

The Tooth Fairy of Inver Grove Heights: "I have this old dog. Gosh, she's gotta be about, oh, 15 years old, and there's some nights when she needs to wake me up and ask to be let out—about 2, 3 in the morning.

"While I'm sitting out here in the dark kitchen, waiting for her to make her stroll around the backyard, sometimes I get into a little nibbling—cookies, crackers, whatever happens to be on the counter. It's important to know that I'm terrifically nearsighted, and I don't always take the time to find my glasses.

"So I was sitting out here in the kitchen, in the middle of the night, in the dark, and I saw this plastic bag of these great big, delicious, salty pretzel rods—and anticipating the first bite, with joy, took a big chomp. And, lo and behold, picked the wrong bag and bit into one of my son's . . . Lincoln Logs. Ouch.

"I don't know many dentists who have had a patient request an immediate appointment because they broke a tooth biting on a Lincoln Log."

Nursing Nancy of Vadnais Heights: "Several years ago, my husband Chris and I met our friends Pat and Pat and their two kids at a restaurant. After dinner, we all went out to the parking lot to admire their new car. Chris chatted outside with the other two adults, while I hopped into the backseat.

"I decided to stick my head out the window to admire the side of the vehicle.

At this very moment, the two kids in the front seat pushed the power window *[BULLETIN BOARD INTERJECTS: Oh, no!]* closed *[BULLETIN BOARD IN-TERJECTS: Aaauuuuggh!]*, effectively slamming the window up onto my neck and closing off my trachea. I could not move, speak or breathe.

"Fortunately, my friend saw my eyes bugging out of my head and quickly got the window open. Once it was all over with, we had an incredible laugh—but I'll tell you what: My trachea was sore every time I swallowed for two days. *[BULLETIN BOARD NOTES: Ours was getting sore even as we listened.]*

"I've never stuck my neck out since."

Twin Sister of Stillwater: "A few years back, my sister Julie came out of the doctor's office wearing a big gauze patch over one eye, because she had a scratch on her cornea. Later on, after a bit of cajoling from me, she told me how it happened.

"It seems that that morning, her mascara was a bit clumpy after it dried—so she took a sewing needle *[BULLETIN BOARD INTERJECTS: Oh, noooooo!]*, proceeded to use it to separate her eyelashes, and inadvertently ended up scratching her eyeball with it.

"I got a lot of mileage out of that one."

Sandy P. of Cottage Grove: "I was just reading about Twin Sister of Still-water—with the cornea and the needle? Oooooooh, ouch. It brought back a memory.

"I think I was in seventh grade; it was junior high, anyway. I was sitting at my little mirror, using one of those eyelash-curler devices, and I was squeez-ing and squeezing, trying to get 'em curly and pretty, when suddenly my el-bow slipped off the edge. Ohhhhhhh. Every last eyelash came out.

"I screamed; my mother came running in; there, in this eyelash curler, were all of my eyelashes.

"I saved them; I still have them in my scrapbook, taped. And now I have a 13-year-old daughter who has one of those eyelash curlers, and when I told her what happened and showed her my eyelashes, she quickly gave it back to me and said: 'No, thanks.' "

Princess Grace of Mahtomedi: "I was a fairly new freshman in the early '70s at the University of Michigan, and I was learning to drink coffee so that I could appear older (which was really stupid) and a lot more cosmopolitan. I was chatting oh-so-wittily with my breakfast companions, and I had ignored some buses that would take me to campus—when I heard the announcement for the last bus that could get me from the north campus to the main campus in time for an important chemistry test.

"I panicked, grabbed my backpack, spilled hot coffee all over those around me, flew out two sets of double doors and suddenly—to my horror—realized that I was quite literally out in space. I'd forgotten that approximately 25 steps separated me from the bus. Those few people on the bus who knew me said I looked like Wile E. Coyote when he runs off a cliff and pauses to gulp before he falls.

"Well, fall I did—cracking my tibia, which is the shin bone, when I landed on my knees. The laughing bus driver waited for me, and I hobbled to class, got a C on my test (which was a real comedown), and—horror of horrors—made my first visit to the student clinic, where the elevator was broken, I had to hop up three flights of stairs to get an X-ray, spent two hours waiting to be examined by a doctor so senile and with such poor eyesight that he walked into the room, patted my bare, outstretched leg at the precise point of the wound and said: 'Well, what seems to be the problem today? Are you here for birth-control advice?'

"It was just a perfect ending to a totally embarrassing day."

Grasshopper of St. Paul: "Years ago, in my misspent youth, I decided to save what was left of a bad evening. There was some champagne left, cheap champagne, in a bottle, and I decided to recork it with the plastic cap that comes on cheap champagne bottles.

"In trying to push the cork into the bottle, I was holding it close to my body, and I got a thin layer of skin on my breast caught in with the cork. I've got to tell you: It's the most horrible thing in the world, because it's funny, it's painful . . . and what are you gonna do? Call the fire department?"

Al of Stillwater: "Back in 1951, my dad was in the Air Force, stationed in Maine on recruiting duty. And believe me: Maine in '51 in the winter was cold—much colder than Minnesota.

"Nowadays, it would be criminal to rent someone a house with no heat in it, but that's the kind of house we had. We bought a gas space heater to heat the house; that was in the living room, and the heat was supposed to seep throughout the house—but the bathroom was the farthest room from the living room, so it was frigid in the middle of winter in that bathroom.

"My parents bought a small electric heater—the kind with a fan inside—and we took it to the bathroom when we took a bath. At the age of 9, at that temperature, you fought like the devil to keep from taking a bath. But anyway: Taking a bath, I got out and just about froze to death while drying off, so I hunkered down in front of that heater . . . squatted down and backed up to it as far as I could—and lo and behold, my rear end contacted the criss-cross front of the grill, and I quickly jumped up.

"For about a year afterwards, I had a criss-cross brand on my rear end, showing my encounter with the heater—which I never showed to anyone other than my parents. If it had been anywhere else, it might have been more embarrassing, but since it was on my rear end and covered by my underwear, no one else knew about it."

Beth of Woodbury: "A few days ago, I sat on the side of the tub to shave my legs. It was a chilly morning, I was scantily clad and I had goose bumps—so I hurried along.

"When I finished, I looked down at my right leg—and it was *covered* with red dots. It looked like an advanced case of chicken pox.

"Upon closer examination, I realized the dots were blood! I had shaved off all of the tiny tips of my goose bumps. And now, as we speak, I have hundreds of tiny scabs all over my right leg.

"Carpe diem."

Don J. of Inver Grove Heights: "A few years ago, as my wife, two teenagers and I were getting our best clothes out and getting ready to go to an important get-together with relatives, we started to run late. It was one of those days, for all of us, that whatever could go wrong, did go wrong.

"Anybody with a home that has only one bathroom can tell you that it got chaotic. Being the last one to get into the bathroom, I checked the time and noticed we should have already been at our destination. Brushing my teeth at supersonic speed, the angle of my arm changed, and I jammed the toothbrush up my nostril to the bridge of my nose.

"The pain of the brush and the sting of the paste was bad enough—but immediately, the blood started to gush out like water over Niagara Falls. I tilted my head back, grabbed a towel to put over my face, pinched my nose and went into the living room to sit down, because I was getting dizzy.

"As tears were running down the side of my face, my kids, very concerned, asked me: 'What happened? All you all right?'

"And, very loudly, I said: 'I shoved a toothbrush up my nose!'

"We did arrive, very late, but only my family had quite a good laugh—and by that time, I was smiling, too.

"I've never brushed my teeth fast again."

Erin of White Bear Lake: "A few years ago, for some odd reason, I let one of our hamsters suck on my chin. I didn't think anything of it—and then, a little while later, I looked in the mirror, and right there, smack-dab in the middle of my chin, was a little black hickey. For about a week or so, I had to wear makeup on my chin and get made fun of by my brothers and sisters and classmates."

Daddy Mark of White Bear Township: "The day after Thanksgiving, I was at my parents' house and playing with my little son. He has a suction-cup basketball hoop, and I thought it'd be funny to stick it to my forehead. I got it to stick—and he started pulling me around by it.

"When I went to take it off, it came off OK—a little bit difficult. I walked out into the other room, where my family was gathered, and everyone started laughing. My wife hollered out: 'What is that? Ink on your head, or what?'

"I went into the bathroom to see if I could wipe it off—and no, it wasn't ink; it was a large hickey. Needless to say, it was a little embarrassing to walk around for the next few days."

The Flipper of Forest Lake: "My husband did the exact same thing a few weeks ago.

"I came home and said: 'What in the heck is that bruise on your forehead?' And here it is, like you said in the paper, the largest hickey I'd ever seen.

"I had to be a little bit thankful that it was a Friday, and he had the whole weekend before he had to go back to work—so they didn't think I was some kind of a weirdo."

John's Wife: "I couldn't believe it when I read about Daddy Mark putting the suction cup on his forehead. I had to read it to my husband, because he did the exact same thing—and I didn't think there could be two people out there that would do such an idiotic thing. We just cracked up laughing.

"And then when I opened the paper and saw that The Flipper had a similar experience, I was just astounded to realize that there were *three* people out there who did the same thing."

Kathee by the Lake: "I know, now, that I married the right guy. As I was reading the Bulletin Board aloud about all of those people out there walking around with suction cups attached to their foreheads, my ever-resourceful and physics-minded husband said: 'Well, why didn't they just get a pin and puncture the cup to release the vacuum?'

"Now, I ask you: Would you have known to do that? I sure wouldn't have."

BULLETIN BOARD REPLIES: You want to see some accidents without mirth? Have a bunch of men with suction cups stuck to their crania start aiming pins at their own foreheads! A big hickey doesn't seem so bad, once you start to think about the alternatives.

Susan of Woodbury: "Several years ago, my husband was shopping at the old Donaldsons at Rosedale—after work, in the winter—and he was wearing a pair of those zip-on rubber Totes over his dress shoes.

"He was riding down the escalator, apparently not paying attention to the world around him, and when he got to the end of the escalator, suddenly he realized that the escalator had caught the toe of his rubber boot—and he couldn't get off the escalator! He was standing there with one foot caught, and people were backing up behind him and stopping to look and laughing, pointing and saying: 'Look! That guy's shoe is getting eaten by an escalator!'

"He tried for several minutes to get his boot loose. Finally he gave up, unzipped the boot—and the escalator sucked the boot up, and it disappeared. He was so embarrassed that he just came home wearing one boot—but being the frugal type, he went back the next day and talked to a manager and received a new boot out of the deal.

"The manager told him this sort of thing happens all the time."

J.N. of Oakdale: "In the category of most embarrassing self-inflicted injury with a golf ball, I offer the following difficult-to-believe but true tale.

"Many years ago, our business sponsored an afternoon of golf for us employees, which, for many of us, was our *only* golf of the year. The first 11 holes were pleasantly uneventful for me, but on hole 12, things got ugly.

"My tee shot was respectably long, and even on the fairway, and my electric golf cart and I were by ourselves as I lined up for shot number two. The swing felt good, but the impact of the golf ball against my lip and teeth a split-second later put an end to the day's golf.

"I had totally toed the shot against the fiberglass cart—10 or so feet away, and directly in front of me—resulting in a perfect return to my face, resulting in the discovery that the blood supply to that part of the body is quite good.

"Surprisingly, only the lip was injured; the underlying teeth held firm. Much as the injury hurt, I'll always remember the feeling of embarrassment about the whole thing.

"Just another data point to suggest that what can happen will happen (to someone)."

CHAPTER 13

The Hat People

*E*arly on in Bulletin Board, **Tony** of Little Canada and **Kathy** of Zimmerman detected, in passing, a connection between the wearing of hats and vehicular incompetence—but the subject did not get its full and proper airing until this exposition by **Merlyn** of St. Paul:

"You know, it's one of those nearly immutable laws of human nature that if you're behind a person on the freeway who stops at the end of the freeway ramp and then proceeds down the freeway at 20 miles an hour in the fast lane, they will be wearing a hat. I don't know if the hat band slows the circulation to the brain, or if the kind of person who wears a hat like that is in a time warp where the rules of the road were different—you know, Hat Land, maybe? Anyway . . .

"I've given up on the usual rude gestures and light-blinking to signal these people. It just confuses them. So, when someone exhibits this behavior *sans* hat, I yell: 'Get a hat!' And if they're hatted, I yell: 'Thanks for the warning!'

"It's not bird-flipping, and they're probably deaf from hat pressure, and I'm sure they don't know what I'm talking about—but at least it's an outlet for my aggression. And, at best, it's a source of embarrassment for my 13-year-old son.

"It's great! Try it sometime."

BULLETIN BOARD REPLIES: And so we shall. We'd like to remind you to be particularly wary of any Hat Person wearing a baseball cap with the visor to the rear—a fashion statement that, in the immortal words of **Bright Spot** *of South St. Paul, is "the universal symbol of a fool."*

Butch of St. Paul: "I saw a Hat Driver this morning—I couldn't believe it—on I-35 going north at 6 o'clock in the morning:

"There's a pickup truck about six feet off the back of a little car, headlights right into the rear window, and he's drivin' along. He's got Yosemite Sam mudflaps on. He's got a gun rack. An American flag in each corner. He's got about a half a load of wood in there. You can see that he's got air fresheners hangin' around in there. It's four-wheel-drive, of course, with the roll bar and what I call 'deer poaching lights.' He's got a bumper rack that says: 'My wife, yes. My dog, maybe. But my gun, never.' On the other side: 'If you don't like my driving, dial 1-800-EAT-S——.' And in the middle, it says: 'My wife's other car is a broom.'

"Watch out, folks. He's there!"

Coyote of St. Paul: "Reading Butch's thing on The Hat People—about that guy who's got that bumper rack that says 'My wife, yes. My dog, maybe. But my gun, never' . . . one of the first times I saw that, I wondered: Does that mean those are the things he'd have sex with? Oh, well. Go figure."

Jay of Minneapolis: "The Hat Phenomenon may be universal.

"The September 18, 1993, issue of *New Scientist,* a British science weekly, had a contest in which readers were asked to predict something that would be discovered by the year 2020.

"According to the magazine, one popular idea was that genes would be discovered that determine popular personality traits. One such trait was described as 'a desire to wear plaid caps (and drive badly).'

"Where have we heard this kind of thing before?

"The reports of readers who have driven on other continents should be encouraged, so that we can find if this is truly universal or only in Minnesota and England."

Jammy of River Falls, Wis.: "Hey! I used to think a lot of winter accidents were caused by poor visibility and slippery roads. Now I find out it's because in the winter, more drivers wear hats.

"I suppose we'll hear: 'The officer found empty headwear at the scene, leading him to believe that the driver was under the influence of a hat at the time of the accident.'

"Could happen."

Joe of the Midway: "I'd just like to thank the Bulletin Board. I'm a cap wearer, and now I have to take my hat off while I'm driving.

"But the good news is: My driving has improved."

And here, with one more reason to eye Hat People with suspicion, is **Mom** *of Cottage Grove:* "This morning, I was reminded of one of the hidden dangers of cold weather. I reached into my closet, which faces an outside wall, and it was extremely cold in there, and it reminded me of what happened last winter:

"I had gotten up, late; rushed my son onto his bus. I was out of, God forbid, cigarettes; I know that's politically incorrect, but anyways . . .

"My hair looked like hell. I had just gotten a bad perm, followed by a worse cut, so I just threw on anything I could find. I was going to go out, once, in that cold weather and then come back and stay home all day.

"So I reached into the ice-cold closet and fished what has to be one of the ugliest winter hats ever created. It looked kind of like a maroon flying saucer with a scarf. Jammed it on my head, ran out to the car, gave it barely enough time for the oil to start flowing through the engine and drove, with teeth chattering, all the way to SA.

"I jumped out of the car and ran into SA. Nice and warm; oh, it felt so *good*. I got a pop, and I got something else, and I was standing in that warm air when all of a sudden . . . the most godawful smell of cat pee assailed my nostrils. And I'm looking around, wondering who . . . the hell . . . in here . . . could stink that bad! And feeling *very* sorry for them—but a little irritated that someone would come to the store reeking of cat urine . . . when suddenly I realized that the other people in line were looking around, but they were all looking at me! And that's when I realized that my darling cat Annie—who happens to be a boy, but once he was neutered, who cares anyway?—had peed on my hat. And in the cold closet, of course the smell was dampened, and then in the warm air of SA, this odor just began to pour out of this hat, but I couldn't take off the hat, 'cause I had this *really* gross haircut on.

"So I just bought my cigarettes, and smiled, and went out and got in my cold car and cried—all the way home.

"Always warm your hat up, and your gloves, if you have a cat—and for God's sake, your shoes!—before you wear them anywhere. You never know."

CHAPTER 14

Fifteen Nanoseconds
of Fame

*B*rushes with the famous:

Jean of Kasota: "It was 1963 or '64. My high-school friend and I were walking home from our routine Saturday afternoon in downtown Mankato when we saw Al Jardine and Mike Love of the Beach Boys heading our way.

PIONEER PRESS FILE PHOTO

"We recognized them and stopped, and they stopped, and we asked them what they were doing there. They said they were in town early for their Sunday-night gig at the Kato Ballroom and thought they'd go to a movie.

"They asked us what was playing, where the theaters were, and how much it cost to get in. We told them 25 cents, and then they asked if they could borrow a quarter. Well, we'd spent our only 35 cents between us on an order of fries and a cherry phosphate. They went on their way, and we went on ours.

"So that's my claim to fame: The Beach Boys tried to bum money off me.

"P.S.: I guess to their credit, the Beach Boys outlasted 25-cent movies, all three downtown-Mankato theaters and the entire city block we met them on, which was a casualty of 'urban renewal.' "

Diana of West St. Paul: "I was med-evaced from Saigon to Bethesda Naval Hospital in Bethesda, Maryland, due to illness contracted while serving in

107

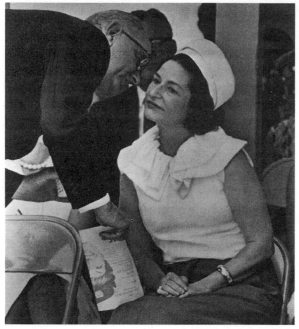

PIONEER PRESS FILE PHOTO

the State Department. I left the war in military-issue pajamas, which—as anyone who's ever been in the military knows—come in three sizes: Large, Huge and Ridiculous.

"They were cobalt blue, and they'd started out with many gripper snappers, all of which were mangled about a thousand times, so that none of them worked. In order to have some modesty, you used two diaper pins down the front of the tunic and as many as you could get for the legs and crotch of the bottoms and in the sides and sleeves of the tunics. Not a pretty sight—especially on a petite female.

"Well, the military is all hung up on rank—and although a civilian, my equivalent rank in the Navy was lieutenant commander, so I was on a female officers' floor with four other female officers, all from the D.C. area. They all had lovely negligees and robes.

"One day—to the everlasting chagrin of the commander head nurse of this floor—the admiral in charge of the hospital, eight Secret Service men, Lady Bird Johnson and Lynda Bird Johnson arrived on the floor to check it out as a birthing place for Lynda Bird in the next month or so.

"By now, you have no doubt guessed who was the *only* patient that the party met. No lipstick, blue rubber thongs and the uniform of the day: blue pajamas and diaper pins. Mrs. Johnson was very gracious and friendly. The commander nearly had a stroke, and I wanted to dig a hole and pull it in after me. Nothing was ever said by the commander, but I still want to dig that hole and pull it in after me—25 years later."

Max of St. Paul: "One of my favorite conservative writers is William F. Buckley, Jr. As chance would have it, I saw him in the airport in Washington,

D.C., a few years back, went up to introduce myself and say hello. He appears more disheveled in real life than he does on television, if you can believe that.

"Lost sight of him—and as it turns out, he got onto the same plane that I did. He rode up in first class. I spent quite a lot of the time craning my neck to try and figure out what it is that William F. Buckley reads; was hoping I might see a *Playboy* magazine stuffed between the pages of some conservative digest.

"When we deplaned, I lost track of him; he was surrounded by a group of people that

PIONEER PRESS FILE PHOTO

met him. I headed toward the men's room, as I always have to do when I get off of a plane—and as I came in, who should be there but William F. Buckley himself. So I went up to the urinal right next to him and said hello again—and to this day, I have been able to tell people that I'm one of the very few people who have won a pissing contest with William F. Buckley, Jr."

Paul of Woodbury, who called just after Conway Twitty's death—and sang so nicely into our answering machine: "I was in the airport in Chicago, going up the escalator, and at the top of the down escalator, here came Conway Twitty with his wife.

"When I got within earshot, I sang: 'People see us everywhere. They think you really care. But my heart I can't deceive . . .'—and I kinda put my hands out, like 'Hit it, Conway,' and he gave a quick little 'I know it's only make-believe.'

"It was really a nice moment; he seemed like a nice guy. Sorry he died."

PIONEER PRESS FILE PHOTO

PIONEER PRESS FILE PHOTO

Geronimo Don: "Back in February of 1945, I was in France as a paratrooper with the 17th Airborne Division. We were training for a combat jump across the Rhine River.

"Marlene Dietrich showed up at the air field, with all the big brass escorting her. We were told that we'd be doing a demonstration jump for her, and we put on our 'chutes and other gear and took off. We bailed out at about 1,000 feet over the drop zone, and I was coming down OK when a sudden change in the wind took me down close to this reviewing group.

"I'd started getting out of my 'chute harness when I noticed someone walking toward me. Lo and behold, it was Marlene herself. She said that was a thrilling event to watch and to tell the men that she was extremely grateful to us for putting on the show for her. She gave me her autograph on my combat jacket and a little peck on the cheek, and said: 'That's for good luck.'

"Later, in combat, I was hit by a fragment from a shell, and it passed right through Marlene's autograph. The good luck she gave me worked, for I was only slightly wounded—but the jacket I was going to save was ruined."

Lois of Mounds View: "In about 1962, I worked at the Twins Motor Hotel on University Avenue. I was about 20 years old, and I did maid work.

"One day, the manager and the head housekeeper called me into the office and said: 'There's a room to clean. It's a celebrity. Go into it, do it right away, and get out. We know you're the only one who isn't gonna go up there and make a fuss.'

"So I went to the room, and I started cleaning. I noticed the person had a bad habit: There were matchbooks all over the room, and there were matches—unlit—thrown all over everywhere: on the floor, on the bed, all over. Well, I couldn't pick up the matches in the vacuum cleaner; I was afraid of a fire, so I got down on my hands and knees and started picking up the matches, one by one.

"Just then, the door opened up. A pair of bare feet came toward me. I looked at the feet, and I didn't know what to do. Then I seen the blue jeans; as I looked up, I seen he had a bare chest. And I looked up to his face, and it was Johnny Cash.

"He said to me: 'I've got a bad habit, don't I, ma'am?' I said: 'Yes, sir, you do.' And I said: 'I'll come back and finish up later.'

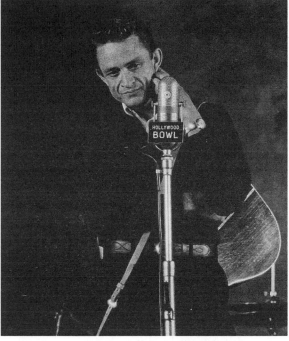

PIONEER PRESS FILE PHOTO

"I walked out of the room, went into the next room, passed out on the bed. They never again asked me to go up and do a celebrity's room."

Beth of White Bear Lake: "Years ago—when Shirley Temple was a young child and very popular—my brother-in-law's mother was working in the bookkeeping department out at Saks Fifth Avenue in Los Angeles. Shirley Temple's mother came in to make a payment on her bill—and Shirley Temple was being an absolute little stinker that day,

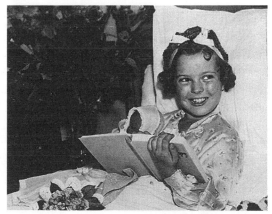

PIONEER PRESS FILE PHOTO

and her mother had just had enough. Her mother spanked her right in front of my brother-in-law's mother. That was her close encounter with a famous

111

person—that she got to see Shirley Temple being a brat and getting a spanking from her mother."

BULLETIN BOARD NOTES: In today's Hollywood, of course, Shirley would have sued her mother for all she was worth.

An Opera Wife of Apple Valley: "When my husband was starting out his opera-singing career, he did some work with the Houston Grand Opera as an apprentice down there— and he got bit on the ear by Leonard Bernstein. Bernstein was gonna come and kiss him on the mouth—he thought—so he turned his head, and instead of Lenny kissing him on the cheek, he bit him in the ear."

PIONEER PRESS FILE PHOTO

PIONEER PRESS FILE PHOTO

Bruce of Oakdale: "When I was a kid, I took private piano lessons from a woman who was Liberace's private piano teacher when he was a kid. She used to give me all these little motivational talks about how I had lots of talent and if I would just practice more conscientiously, I could grow up to be just like Liberace. When I turned about 12 and finally saw Liberace and realized what that meant, I immediately quit lessons."

Paul of Maplewood: "You had a story recently about a fellow whose parents ended up helping pull John Dillinger out of a ditch one day and realized it later when they saw his picture in the paper.

"Well, my grandmother, who grew up in central Wisconsin, used to tell of how, when she was in her late 20s, she and a friend were out berry-picking in a rather deserted area along a county road, and this fellow stopped and asked them if they would come to his farm—saying he needed some help doing something or another.

PIONEER PRESS FILE PHOTO

"They took a look at him, and he just didn't seem quite right. They ended up getting in their car and hightailing it out of there. It wasn't too much later when they saw his picture in the paper. The fellow was Ed Gein, the fellow who did taxidermy on human beings.

"If my grandmother had gone with Ed Gein that day, I might not be here to call you now."

World Traveler of St. Paul: "My brush with fame happened at the Minneapolis–St. Paul airport in August of the summer before last.

"I was trying to fly out to Maine, via Boston, with my 8-week-old son, to join my husband, who had flown out the day before. The flight to Boston was late in departing, so all the passengers were waiting at the gate to find out when we would be leaving. A few seats over from me, I noticed a man wearing glasses and holding a very large magazine. It turned out the man was blind and was reading a Braille edition of *Playboy* magazine. I thought to myself that I had actually come across a man who really was reading *Playboy* for the articles.

"The man looked vaguely familiar, and then I realized that I was looking at Ray Charles.

113

PIONEER PRESS FILE PHOTO

"Shortly after my bright realization, it was announced that the flight to Boston was canceled. I was pondering the mechanics of getting back to the house with my infant, a large suitcase, and all the other stuff you carry around when you travel with a baby, when I heard Mr. Charles ranting to his traveling companions that they'd better find *some* flight to *somewhere* to get him out of 'the middle of nowhere.'"

BULLETIN BOARD MUSES: It's just great to be here in the Twin Cities again. And hey, you've been a wonderful audience.

Bee of St. Paul: "Many years ago, my friend and I were shopping at Dayton's downtown, and in walked the most beautiful woman, with what appeared to be a small entourage around her. They were all standing at the makeup counter—so my friend and I got closer for a look. The person who seemed to be her assistant—a man—saw us and said: 'Yes, that's her. It's Geraldine Chaplin. Would you girls like her autograph?' We said: 'Well, sure!' She even spoke to us; said 'Hi' or something.

"So we received our autographs and walked away, and as soon as we got some distance away from them, my friend and I looked at each other and said: 'Who? Who the heck was that?'"

PIONEER PRESS FILE PHOTO

114

CHAPTER 15

The Sign on the Road to the Cemetery Said "Dead End"

Laughter on the roadway:

Maria of Highland Park: "In Evanston, Illinois, there was a senior citizens' center on one side of the street and a cemetery on the other side of the street—and seriously, there was a big yellow sign that said: 'Slow Down. Senior Citizens Crossing.'"

The Parkers of Roseville: "We saw a sign on the edge of Roseville Cemetery: 'We are expanding to meet our community's needs.'"

Neil of Amery, Wis.: "I grew up in a little town in northern Iowa—not too far from West Bend, which is the home of the world-famous West Bend grotto. The town's probably less than a thousand people, and there was a hotel just on the outside of town—one of these old-fashioned motels—and it must have had a real optimistic proprietor, because the sign outside the motel said: 'Stay 6 Nights; Get Your 7th Night Free.'"

The Wordsmith of St. Paul: "On West Seventh Street today, I saw a flower shop with a sign out front advertising 'Fall Bokays.' I wonder if this could be a result of too many people learning to read from Hooked on Phonics."

Tony of Minneapolis: "I work at the U of M, and the other day I saw something that made me think of Bulletin Board. It was a parking meter that said: 'Quarters Only. 90 Cents Per Hour.' I will refrain from further comment."

Rose of St. Paul: "The funniest sign I ever saw was in San Francisco. At the bottom of this really, really steep hill, there was a sign that said: 'Hill.' And somebody wrote under it: 'No S—.'"

Louise of the East Side: "Saw a pretty nifty sign out here on the East Side, on a muffler shop. It reads: 'Don't Call for an Appointment. We'll Hear You Coming.'"

Ken of Shoreview: "Sign on shop in St. Paul: 'Car Radio Repair. Drive In—Have Your Radio Repaired While You Wait And Wait And Wait.'"

Rex Twiss of St. Paul (and a bunch of other callers): "The funniest sign that I ever saw was one painted on the side of a radiator-repair shop on Lake Street in Minneapolis. It said: 'A Good Place To Take A Leak.'"

Marge of St. Paul: 'In Las Vegas, leaving the city, there's a sign that says: 'Have One For The Road—And We'll Provide The Chaser.'

Jo of parts unknown: "Many years ago, as we approached the eastern border of Ohio, we saw a sign that said 'Last Chance To Buy Gas At 24.9 Cents Per Gallon.' (I did say that it was many years ago.) Anyway, we filled up with gas. Upon entering West Virginia, it was true—it was our last chance to buy gas at 24.9 cents per gallon. In West Virginia, it was 22.9 cents."

Peter of parts unknown: "I worked for Alcan Aluminum in Kitimat, British Columbia. Kitimat is a city built in a valley, and up on the side of the valley, beside the road on the way out of the valley, there's a church, a somewhat impressive church. It's the First United Church of Kitimat. And they constructed a large sign beside their church, in the parking lot, back in the early '60s. This was a sign maybe 30 feet high. The first letters were capitalized except the first letter of 'of,' and the rest of the sign was printed in smaller print, so if you stood down in the town and looked up there at the church, you can imagine what you saw.

"It stayed for two or three weeks, and then the entire sign disappeared. One can't help but wonder: Who told the pastor?"

Howard Cameron of Osceola, Wis.: "The best sign I've ever seen was at Yosemite National Park by a waterfall. It said: 'If You Slip And Fall, You Will Die.' No cutting any corners on that sign."

Tina of St. Paul: "We went to the Mall of America last weekend, and there's a food stand there called Everything Turkey. Right underneath the sign for the restaurant is a big neon sign that says: 'Fresh Squeezed Juices.' Yuck."

Jack of Long Lake: "Punctuation is so important.

"The chalkboard menu in a Rice Lake, Wisconsin, restaurant read:

"Soups of the Day:

"Cr. of Broccoli

"Veg. Beef

"Chicken Dump

"Somehow the Chicken Dump didn't sound too appealing to me."

Renee of Arden Hills: "A few years ago, when my daughter lived in San Antonio, Texas, she used to travel back and forth on the train—and somewhere out there in the hinterlands was a sign that tickled her. It said: 'Fred's Fried Chicken & Auto Repair.' We've often wondered about Fred's recycling procedures."

Lavender Lil of Crocus Hill: "There's a hardware store on West Seventh in St. Paul, and they have a sign in the window that says '40,000 Items On The Floor.' Sounds like sort of a dangerous spot to me."

Marv of Inver Grove Heights: "This is a sign I saw in a beer joint down in Mobile, Alabama, when I was in the service: 'In Case Of An Air Raid, Crawl Under The Pot. No One's Hit It Yet.' "

CHAPTER 16

This 'n' That 'n' the Other

There's no better way to say it. Here's some of this 'n' that 'n' the other:

Biology lesson: From **Bea** of West St. Paul:

"It was many years ago, on the morning before Easter. We looked out the kitchen window, and there was a rabbit in the backyard, under the lilac bush.

My husband surreptitiously took a hard-boiled egg out of the bowl I had them hiding in, on top of the refrigerator. It was a pale yellow egg. He went out in the backyard and approached the bunny rabbit, which scampered away. My husband reached down to the ground, picked the egg up, and with an 'Ohhhh!' look on his face, he held it up for the children to see.

"My next-door neighbor also was looking out her kitchen window, and she saw this happening. 'Jack!' she called to her husband. 'Jack, do rabbits lay eggs?' He laughed at her and said: 'Oh, no, of course not.' And she said: 'But I just saw one!' "

Freaks of nature: From **Bob Woolley** of St. Paul:

"Several years ago, there was a great article in the magazine called *Whole Earth Review* about the amount of stupidity in the world. It gave several general rules. The first rule was: There is always more stupidity in the world than you think. The second rule is: Even after you take Rule 1 into account, there is *still* always more stupidity in the world than you think.

"My second observation is a specific example of this fact: Yesterday, I went to the State Fair, and while wandering around through the Midway, I came across an exhibit which, if it has been there before, I have somehow overlooked. The displays on the outside show a beautiful young woman with a tragic story: Apparently, she was a centerfold model who was in a horrible car accident and was decapitated. Fortunately, however, she was rushed to a nearby research hospital, where doctors managed to preserve her life—even with her head completely severed—and she has been maintained on this artificial life support for the last several years. With no head.

"Now, I don't for a second believe this—any more than I believe that there is a Loch Ness Monster or that there are Potato People or that space aliens have recently been changing their allegiance from Ross Perot to Bill Clinton. But I'm intensely curious as to what, exactly, there is that one can see for 80 cents' worth of coupons. I'm not curious enough—at this point, anyway—to spend 80 cents to see it, so I figure I will do the next-best thing and ask somebody who has seen it.

"And as I'm staring at the trailer . . . sure enough, a young man pays his fare, steps up to the window, looks for a while and steps down. So I decide to ask him.

"I say: 'What *is* in there?'

"He goes: 'Uhhh, it's a woman with no head.'

"I say: 'No. What is it *really?*'

"He says: 'Uhhh, it's a woman sitting in there, and she has no head.'

"I said: 'Yeah, but . . . but . . . how are they making it *look* like that?'

"He goes: 'Whattya mean, look like that? I mean, it's a woman without a head!'

"It's clear to me at this point that he really believes this.

"So I wonder whether somebody who actually *has* a head, but doesn't use it, is, in any significant sense, any better off than a woman who doesn't have a head."

Modesty today: An eyewitness account by **Mrs. Mac** of Circle Pines:

"I'm in Rosedale tonight, shopping, and there's this young man *patiently* waiting outside the shoe store for his girlfriend. She's in there trying on shoes.

"She's got this skimpy little halter top on; her chest is half sticking out, and her entire stomach is showing. So she's half-naked, and she walks back out of the shoe store and says to her boyfriend: 'I didn't like those shoes. I don't want my *toes* showing!'

"I thought: 'For God's sake, lady, everything else on your body is showing. Why not your toes, too?'

"Made my night."

Brave New Bod: On how we might re-engineer the human machine, from **Marge** of St. Paul (a topic we discussed *long* before the Bobbitt trial, in case you're wondering):

"I think we need to have snaps installed in women's shoulders; that way, our purses, bras and slips would stay in place. It'd make life a lot easier.

"The second thing, which I think would save marriages, relationships throughout the world: Make a certain part of the male anatomy detachable! That way, when the guy leaves the house, the woman could just take it off and put it in a drawer and know exactly where it is."

Muse, amuse: From **Guinevere** of Afton:

"I'd like to reveal what I do to entertain myself when I'm stuck in a boring gathering. I once read in a psychology magazine that one out of every 50 people has committed bestiality. So I like to figure out which person or persons in the gathering has done it with an animal. If I'm really bored, I envision what kind of an animal they've been intimate with. It's a great way to keep from looking bored."

Hmmmmmmmmmmm: And feel free to hmmmmmmmmmm along:

Diane of Forest Lake: "I just got back from a trip up to the store. I probably went about three miles, total. Along the way, at three different places, there was a shoe along the side of the road. Three different times. Which makes me wonder: How does one lose a shoe? Does somebody absently put it on the top of their car, like a hot cup of coffee, and drive away? Does a kid open a window and throw it out? Or does it drop off your foot while you're walking and you don't know it?"

LaLa of St. Paul: "Why is it that the men who send you flowers are men you want to be platonic with?"

Robert of St. Paul: "I work in a retail store, and on occasion, we ask people if they need help. They inevitably answer: 'No, just killing time.' And I've always wondered if they realize that time is killing them quicker than they're killing it."

Janet of St. Paul: "Is it just me that thinks it weird? Right next to the morgue in St. Paul, there's a picnic table and a barbecue grill."

Sue of Woodbury: "I just got finished sweeping the real cobwebs off the front of my house, so that I could put up the fake cobwebs that my kids wanted for Halloween. Does that make sense?"

Frodo of Shoreview: "I have a conundrum: We have a cat, and if you take the cat and hold him by his legs about a foot off the floor and drop him, he's gonna land on his feet, right? They always land on their feet.

"Well, when I'm in the kitchen buttering some toast, and I happen to drop it, it seems like it always drops buttered side down.

"I'm just wondering: If you took a piece of buttered toast and strapped it to the back of a cat . . . well, you get what I mean."

David Stever of St. Paul: "It's Saturday, and I'm participating in manly pursuits: I'm watching football on TV. And I noticed that the U.S. Marine Corps has an ad in which they portray our nation's enemies, I guess, as pieces on a chess board. The Marine Corps hero pursues the black bishop all over the board. The movement of the Marine Corps hero across the board indicates that he's a queen, but I suppose no one can ask him whether or not he's a queen."

K.C. of Cottage Grove: "Our office got new chairs today, and on the first line of the instructions, it says: 'WARNING: USE THIS PRODUCT ONLY FOR SEATING ONE PERSON AT A TIME.' It kinda makes you wonder what's going on behind closed doors of offices if they need to put that kind of instruction on chairs."

Some good news, some bad news: From **The Fabulous Julie Flame** of the West Side:

"Talk about upsetting things. I had to go to my doctor today for my bad back, and he gave me some pills. And he says, 'You will probably have to take these for the rest of your life.'

"He gave me enough pills to last for nine days."

Not exactly what they had in mind: From an **anonymous woman**:

"I work at Wal-Mart, and I think it's kind of funny that they play the song 'Take This Job and Shove It' over the PA system while we're working—and we're all singing along to it."

And from **Rich** of Highland Park: "A few days ago, my wife and I were driving in a major city west of the Mississippi River—I'll leave it nameless—and we noticed a sign that said 'Medusa.' We were saying: 'Wonder what that is'—and as we drove closer, we realized it was a hair salon.

"Well, we just cracked up. Whoever started this company probably was asleep during Greek mythology. Think about this: What image do you get from Medusa? Yeah, sure, somebody's gonna come in and say: 'Oh, gee, I wanna come in here so my head'll look like snakes are sprouting from it! And when anybody looks at me, they'll turn to stone! And then, let's see, somebody's gonna come around and chop my head off!'

"What possessed these people to name a hair salon Medusa? What's next—Icarus Airlines?"

When cultures collide: From **Tom** of White Bear Lake:

"A college friend told me this first-day-on-the-job story about his sister, a nursing student who was doing some work at a clinic.

"She went into the waiting room and read off a name: 'Jesus [Hispanic surname]. Jesus [Hispanic surname]. Is there a Jesus [Hispanic surname] here?'

"A man came up to her and kind of shyly said: 'It's Hay-SOOSE. Hay-SOOSE.'

"She just said: 'Well, it says Jesus here.'"

BULLETIN BOARD REPLIES: Let's call the whole thing off.

Gaining something in translation: From **Dannae** of St. Paul:

"I was in Taiwan a few years ago on a cultural exchange, and a Taiwanese friend who was my host took me to a market.

"To my great pleasure, in the market I found several garments—mostly Hawaiian-style shirts—that were printed with English-language phrases. The one that caught my eye was a shirt that said: 'Tweak the nose of a deer at 2 P.M.' The market was filled with these totally off-the-wall English sayings that made no sense, and I was laughing really hard.

"My host asked me what was so funny, and I told him that the English phrases on the shirts were totally off-the-wall and just wonderful. He started laughing, and he said: 'See that blond-haired man over there?' It was another tourist in the market, and he was wearing a T-shirt with this beautiful Chinese calligraphy on the front. I thought: At least that shirt had some taste; it was graphically beautiful.

"He said: 'Do you know what that guy's shirt says?'

"And I said: 'No.'

"And he said: 'It says: "I am for sale." We can always pick out the Americans.'

"So I don't *quite* get it—but it was a joke on *both* sides."

Mee-owwwwwww! From the sharp-eyed **Pam** of St. Paul:

"I work at a company that makes labels, and I was working on a label for a dog-food company.

"The customer sends, over the fax, the ingredients that he wants on the label. I send it into typesetting, and it comes back out to me, and it's my job to proofread the label. So I'm reading along—you know, brewer's rice, poultry by-product meal, corn gluten meal, ground cats . . . I went: 'Ground cats? Wait a minute!'

"So I looked on the fax, and it was supposed to be ground oats, but the 'o' didn't come through too clearly on the fax, so it looked like a 'c.' I'm kinda glad I caught that one."

BULLETIN BOARD REPLIES: As are cats everywhere.

Mixed messages: From **Michelle** of New Brighton:

"I had just turned north on Hennepin from Lake Street. Traffic was surrounding me as I slowed for the red light a few blocks north on Hennepin. Just then, a little car zoomed up next to me, and the woman driving had her head and fist out the window, with her face all red, yelling to me that I was driving too slow. She was so worked up about it that she appeared ready to shoot someone.

"As she lane-jockeyed over to turn off Hennepin, everyone in the car got a huge laugh as we read the bumper sticker on her car: VISUALIZE WORLD PEACE."

Kevin of Woodbury: "I took the kids to the circus Sunday. The first act is the lions; they come out in their cages, and the ringmaster is cracking his whip—and obviously, these lions aren't having any fun at all. And what does the orchestra start playing? 'Born Free'!"

Instant perennials: From **Ragbrai** of parts hereabouts:

"The other day, my sister and I decided that we needed a change in the garden, so we went out and bought fake flowers and planted them in our garden. We've gotten lots of compliments on our wonderful flowers."

Finders, losers: From **Merlyn** of St. Paul:

"I was at the farmers' market the other day, buying some vegetables, and as I went to pay the woman selling stuff, a dime fell out of my coin purse onto the ground.

"A little girl rushed over and picked it up. I thought: 'Oh, well. I'll let her think she found a dime.'

"But as I turned to walk on, I heard her say to her mother: 'Look what I found!' Her mother said: 'This must be your lucky day!' And the girl said: 'Yeah. That lady dropped it, but I ran over and grabbed it before she could pick it up!'

"I expected the mother's response to be something like: 'Oh, if you know who dropped it, you should give it back'—at which point I would say, 'Oh, you keep it—for being honest.'

"Instead, she said: 'We're having black beans and rice for supper, OK?'"

"The kid gained a dime—and her mother lost a chance at one of those million-dollar lessons in life.

"Well, you can't be the mom to the world, but today I felt sad for this kid and her sister, who learned the *wrong* lesson—and it cost me a dime, to boot."

The thrill of victory: A tale of the competitive spirit, from **Becca** of Forest Lake:

"Last month, during a softball tournament, I was taking a bathroom break at McDonald's. When I was finishing up, two girls from another team came in. While I was washing my hands, I heard, 'One, two, three—go.' Then:

" 'Done.'

" 'No, I was done first.'

"They were having a peeing race!

"These are people with too much time on their hands."

Two-way radio: From the long-lost **Judge Crater** of St. Paul:

"I'm going to take you back to the very early 1930s—perhaps 1930 or 1931, when radio broadcasting was certainly a novelty, and when children were not as sophisticated as they are today.

"I was in the living room of my parents' house, with the big old box radio— the one that stood on the floor and towered over you—and I was listening to the radio one afternoon with my cousin. My cousin was . . . oh, I don't know, maybe about 13; I was about 4 or 5, and he was listening to a program. It was almost time for one of *my* favorite programs, so I went over to the radio—after all, it was in *our* home—and moved my hand up to turn the radio dial.

"He said: 'What are you going to do?'

"I said: 'I'm going to turn to a different station.'

"And he said: 'Aw, gee, don't do *that!* If you turn to a different station, the people that are on the air now will feel just terrible.'

"I said: 'What?'

"And he said: 'Well, they'll know that you're turning them off! And they'll feel just terrible. So don't do *that!*'

"I sat there and looked in wonder at that radio, for hours. And for months and months and months after that, whenever I was going to change the station, I would turn it off so that nobody would know what was going on. Then I would carefully adjust the radio dial and turn it back on again—and that kept everybody happy. It kept me happy, and it didn't offend the people who were broadcasting."

That's pathetic! Here's **Connie S.** of Bloomington, who combined two of our discussions (children's television and bird droppings) and came up with something entirely different:

"I grew up in South Dakota, where we watched 'Captain 11' on Channel 11—what an odd coincidence!—out of Sioux Falls. He was dressed up in like an airline-pilot costume; it was supposed to be a spaceship. The kids in the studio who were having a birthday got to go up to the big panel and flick a switch, and then a cartoon would come on.

"We lived about 70 miles from Sioux Falls. I didn't think the chances were very good that I'd ever make it to the TV studio, so we invented our own version of Captain 11 to play at home. We had a metal swing set, and it kind of . . . attracted bird droppings. What we would do is look for the dried bird droppings, and then we would take turns and pretend that we were on 'Captain 11'; we would flick off a dried bird dropping, and that would start a cartoon in our imaginations, and we'd act out the cartoon.

"So I was sharing this memory with a friend, thinking that it was really an inventive variation of creating our own TV show—and a really cool thing—and he looked at me and said: 'That is the most pathetic thing I have ever heard in my life.' In retrospect, maybe it was pretty weird, but it was really fun. We *thought* we were having fun."

Life imitates art: From **Dandy Dave, the Mendota Mensch**, reporting on a visit to the Walker Art Center in Minneapolis:

"At an exhibit which consisted of a bar and an artfully—and realistically—posed bartender and patron, I spied a blue chair which faced a television set. There was a sign: 'Please feel free to sit in the blue chair.' So, I did.

"Sitting there, weighted down with outerwear and whatnot, watching a videotape, I was unconsciously drumming the fingers of my right hand on my right knee. A man with three small children in tow approached and said quietly, 'Look, kids! His fingers are moving!' Then after just enough time for a double take, he almost screamed: 'He's ALIVE!'

"It's the only time I've been mistaken for a work of art."

BULLETIN BOARD MUSES: One more time than most of us.

Sign's of the time's: From **Ace** of Wyoming:

"I believe I'll start the Apostrophe Redistribution Center. All of those businesses with an apostrophe in their signs or their ads where it doesn't belong? We will collect them and give them to all of those businesses with signs and ads where they do belong. Our commission will be small—like a comma, or maybe even just a period. This could be extremely lucrative."

New word orders: Here's a fax from **Ted & Joe,** "two misguided kids from St. Louis Park who grew older but never grew up" that we ran on Election Day—Tuesday, November 3rd, 1992:

"After seeing the movie *Sneakers,* we got to discussing the topic of anagrams (a word or phrase formed by reordering another word or phrase), which were featured in the opening of the movie. We hit upon the following, perhaps prophetic, anagrams:

"Ronald Wilson Reagan: INSANE ANGLO WAR LORD

"Ross Perot: SORE SPORT or, better yet, S.S. TROOPER

"Tuesday, November Third: MANY VOTED, BUSH RETIRED"

BULLETIN BOARD NOTES: You may decide for yourself how many Ted & Joe got right.

The wisdom of youth: From **Sandy** of Marine:

"At Christmas, we were sitting around my father-in-law's house, and he was telling us how at Thanksgiving, his grandson (my nephew) was staying with him for a few days, and one of the jobs my father-in-law had to do was go out to this farm and castrate pigs. He took Josh with him, and after the day was done and they were back sitting around the kitchen table before suppertime, my father-in-law asked Josh what they thought about the job that they had done that day.

"And Josh said, with absolutely no humor in his voice: 'I'm glad I'm not a pig.' "

The wisdom of age: From **Lillian Crandall** of Circle Pines:

"We just came back from shopping, and there was a car ahead of us driven by a very prim and proper little old white-haired lady, and she had a bumper sticker that read: 'Screw The Golden Years.' "

The merry pranksters: From **Grandma Up North:**

"My husband said that it would be so much fun to rent a panel truck and put 'Publishers' Clearinghouse Prize Patrol' on there and drive it up and down the streets. Well, we only have two streets here, but anyway, he says: 'Could you imagine: *Who's it for? Who's it for?*' ' "

126

Oh, any time! No, any time! From **Receptionist** of White Bear Lake—and we truly wish you could have *heard* the years of frustration spilling past her lips in this memorable rant:

"I get hundreds of calls a week; people want to schedule appointments to come in. That's fine. I say: 'Do you want morning or afternoon?' And they say: 'Oh, well, I have the day off! Any . . . any time is fine. I can come any time!'

"And I say: 'Well, I can do, like, a 2 o'clock or a 3 o'clock this afternoon.' And they say: 'Oh, don't you have anything this *morning*? I'm not *available* this afternoon.'

"You just want to *shake* people and say: 'You said *any time* was fine; you're off all day—and then you say you can't come at that time! *Why* did you say you were available . . . any . . . time?'

"People, when you schedule appointments and you're asked 'Do you want morning, or do you want afternoon?' please say one or the other. Don't tell me any time is fine, and then I give you a time and you say you can't come. That is really, *really* aggravating.

"You do this 40 hours a week, five days a week, every day, three hun—. . . how many days a year? You just get really sick and tired of people saying 'Oh, any time is fine'—because any time is *not* fine with everybody. It doesn't work that way.

"Thank you for letting me get that—*finally!*—off . . . I guess you could say my chest; I don't care what you say. But . . . *auugh!* I have wanted to say that to people for so many *years* now, and they just don't *get* it! *Auugh!* Thank you, Bulletin Board."

BULLETIN BOARD REPLIES: Any time. No, really!

After the beep: From **Hammerhead Tom** of St. Paul:

"The best phone message I ever had on my answering machine went as follows: 'Hi. This is Tom. I can't come to the phone right now, but . . . uhhh-hhh . . . uhhhhhh . . . hang on a second; I'll get a sheet of paper and a pencil here . . . OK, I'm ready now. What's the message?' "

Boy, did they get the wrong number! From **Riley** of Maplewood:

"In another town, my number was one digit different from a local bar. My last two digits were 9-3; the bar was 3-3, and all the other numbers were the same.

"This one lady kept calling me back one night, four times in a row, wanting to speak to her husband, Joe. I kept telling her she had the wrong number; of course, my teenage daughter was playing rock music in the background, and she swore up and down that it was not the wrong number.

"So finally, the last time she called, I pretended to be the bar. I yelled out: 'Joe! Telephone!' And I told her he refused to come to the phone. She said: 'Well, he better. It's his wife.' And I said: 'Joe! It's your wife!' I said: 'Joe doesn't want to talk to you.' She says: 'Well, he better.' I kept pretending I was relaying the messages to Joe and Joe kept refusing to talk to her. The end result was: She says, 'Boy, wait 'til he gets home.'

"I've wondered, for the last 10 to 15 years since I did this, what happened to poor Joe when he got home."

Nocturnal emissions: A strange utterance in the middle of the night, remembered by **Debbie** of Inver Grove Heights:

"About 10 years ago, my husband and I were living in a house that didn't have air conditioning; we had to keep the doors open so the air could go through the screens. Of course, nowadays you'd be afraid you were gonna get murdered or mugged or something. But we had these door stops, and one night he sat up in bed and said: 'We've gotta *name* those door stops.' And I thought: 'Good grief.' "

Today's helpful hint: From **Dorothy** of St. Paul:

"I'm an older lady. My husband was never much of one to go out and eat, and I want to tell you how I parlayed a pound of liver into occasional excursions out for supper.

"I would take the container of liver out to thaw, and in his going through the kitchen, he would end up saying: 'Ugh. What are we going to have for supper?'

"And I would mention the liver. And it wasn't very long before he'd say, 'Gee, whiz, can't you put that back and maybe we can go out for supper?'

"Sure. Y'know, it would be still partly frozen, and I'd put it back. I parlayed that into at least a half-dozen trips out. When I didn't want to cook, I'd haul that liver out—and the same scenario, again and again. It was great.

"It's kind of devious, but I'd suggest it to any young bride."

BULLETIN BOARD ADDS: Or groom, of course, this being the '90s.

Truly scary thoughts: From **Kathy** of Maplewood:

"A while back, my mom pointed out that in 30 or 40 years, nursing homes are going to be full of people named Debbie and Kathy and all of those other popular names of the '50s. And then I thought: 'Oh, my God! The kitchen bands!'

"Now, don't get me wrong, because I think kitchen bands are wonderful—

but just how well are the classics of our youth going to translate to pots and pans? I mean: 'House of the Rising Sun' or 'Louie, Louie'—think about it! It's scary!

"I hope some of us remember to save our guitars."

Life after death: From **Doctor Friendly** of St. Paul:

"I was looking over a patient's health-insurance policy, to find out whether a procedure we were thinking about doing would be covered or not. It has a section labeled 'Services We Do Not Cover.' The statement under that is: 'If you get these services, you will have to pay for them.'

"The first item on the list is Autopsies.

"This has to be the ultimate in adding insult to injury. First you die. Then, they cut you up. Then, they send you a bill for it."

Penny foolish: From **W.T.** of Rochester:

"When I was 16 years old, in 1932, I took a job in a small garage owned by 'Otto.' The pay rate was either 25 cents or 35 cents an hour, depending on the kind of work assigned. I had to be at the job 48 hours a week, but only got paid for actual hours worked. Some days I would be on the job for eight hours but only be paid for two; it depended on if and when customers might show up to have repairs made.

"The time sheet showed I was to be paid $5.35 for my first week of work. Otto studied the work sheet for a long time. Finally he said, 'Well, we will just call that $5 even.' I thought to myself, 'Who is this *we* that decided I was to get 35 cents less?' This was during the Depression time, when prices were low. That 35 cents would have bought seven hamburgers or hot dogs, or frosty root beers, or fountain Cokes.

"A previous employee, Burt, told me he wanted to find out how cheap Otto could be. The garage had one of those pits in the floor where you stood to work on the underside of a car. Burt placed a penny on the floor when Otto was not watching. While working in the pit, Otto spied the penny and could not reach it. Otto crawled out from the grease pit, walked over and picked up the penny, took his twist-top coin purse out of his pocket, deposited the penny, and crawled back into the grease pit.

"Otto loved to make money and keep it. It bothered him to spend even small amounts. I saw him from time to time through the years. He became investment-smart and wore a blue business suit. I think he had the same suit for the last 20 years of his life. He lived past 90, and it was rumored that he died a millionaire. How lucky can a person get?"

BULLETIN BOARD REPLIES: Not lucky enough to take it with him.

CHAPTER 17

Reckless Abandoned

*W*hen *did you know your youth was all spent? That was the question, as posed by* **Dr. V.** *of St. Paul:*

"About a week ago, I turned out of one of the University of Minnesota's parking ramps onto Ontario Street and noticed that the little house between the ramp and the corner grocery had disappeared: nothing left but a vacant lot. That was the house where a friend decided to introduce me to alternative rock by the simple method of playing CDs from 9:30 at night until dawn the next morning—sort of like brainwashing.

"Now there's no sign that anything was ever there, and if it weren't for the stack of alternative tapes in my car, I'd seriously wonder if I'd hallucinated my entire wild youth. Certainly, I'll never be quite that young and stupid again.

"So I wondered when (or if) other people had noticed that adolescence was gone forever, and what they'd thought about it."

Michael of Owatonna: "Who *is* this guy 'reminiscing' about those long-ago days when he was introduced to alternative rock on CD? Don't you have to be a few miles down the road of life before you qualify to lament your lost youth? CDs, for crying out loud! I still have Beatles albums in mono—and never thought about lost adolescence until my kid got her driver's license."

Don Jones of Cottage Grove: "I got onto an elevator one day, and the Beatles were playing on the Muzak."

Jeni of Hastings: "I'm only 16, and I already feel old—because Time-Life has a record out where I can recognize almost all of the songs! I can't believe it!"

Dr. Doom of St. Paul: "I realized my better days were long gone when I walked into the bathroom and found my beloved wife tweaking out a few chin hairs with my old roach clip."

The Desk of Leonard Smalls, Stuttgart on Mississippi: "Leonard realized that he was old when it took longer to clean up before his parties than after."

130

Pat of St. Paul, on a Saturday morning: "I realized last night that I'm getting old. I'm only 28, but after we went out to a local bar and we left at 11:30, I said to the person I was with: 'You know, I have a heck of a lot more fun when I go to Rainbow on a Friday night, maybe hit Target and pick up something, and then we go to Dairy Queen and are home by 10.' It's kinda sad, isn't it?"

The same **Pat** of St. Paul, on that Sunday morning: "After I hung up yesterday, I started thinking about what I said, and then I was reading all the stories for that woman named A.J. *[a 19-year-old addict struggling to stay sober, who'd asked Bulletin Board's readers for guidance]*, and I woke up this morning and thought: I started having fun (going to Rainbow, etc.) with my friends when I quit drinking and smoking, a year ago January, and I realized that that *is* fun; it's not sad at all, because I now have control of my life, and I come home and I'm sober, and I feel good, and I wake up and have a clear head, and I have a wonderful weekend ahead of me—instead of gettin' drunk all day Saturday, and gettin' drunk again on Sunday at the football game.

"So I guess I realized that it's not sad at all."

P.J. of White Bear Lake: "A friend and I were out antiquing the other day in some shops in the area—and we both saw dishes that we had received as wedding gifts."

Cathy of Eagan: "My husband and I, who are both still in our 20s, went to Disneyland about a year and a half ago and realized we were getting old—because 1) we were concerned about the high price of getting in; 2) we didn't go on the water ride because we thought we might get wet; and 3) we left before the light parade, because we knew we had a long ride back to his parents' house, which was about two hours away."

Walt of Wayzata: "Without any prodding from either of my parents, I made my own dentist appointment. That was when I knew it was all over."

Eighth-grader of Eagan: "I realize that I'm getting older. For my 13th birthday, I got a pair of white tennis shoes. My birthday was over a month ago, and my shoes are still white."

Phil of St. Paul: "I knew I was getting old when I found my college track spikes in the attic—and the first thing I thought was: These would be great for aerating the backyard."

Andy of Eagan: "My wife and I just bought a vacuum cleaner—and it was the highlight of our week. . . . So sad."

Dahlia of Lexington: "I had a child when I was just a teenager, and I knew I was all grown up when, for my 18th birthday, my parents' gift to me was a high chair."

Chris of Stillwater: "It really hit hard. It was 1972. That April, I had gotten married. That May, I had graduated from high school. And that August, I gave birth to my baby. And in the mail I got cards of congratulations—many from my girlfriends who, after graduation, had decided to spend the summer in Florida, working as cocktail waitresses in the evening, sleeping on the beach all day. I remember reading that and looking at my infant son and realizing I'd never be able to do that. My youth was gone, and I never got it back."

Ruthanne of St. Paul: "The other day, I was talking to my dad about noticing how I'm getting older and how it seems like all these people who are in the checkout lanes and waitressing and stuff like that . . . how when I was little, they seemed so old, and now they seem so young. They're just kids, mostly.

"And my dad looks me straight in the eye and says: 'You think that's bad? Just wait 'til there's a president younger than you are.' "

Laurie of St. Paul: "Clinton was on TV talking about the national health-care plan—and I didn't turn it off. I sat and listened to the . . . whole . . . thing."

Nancy of St. Paul: "We had a party with a bunch of college friends fairly soon after we graduated—and we spent a good 45 minutes to an hour discussing our health-care benefits."

Gale of Stillwater: "While I was cashiering the other day, two little girls—around age 9 or 10—brought a coupon for free candy to the register. I told them they'd have to pay the three cents tax, and I made the comment that 'Uncle Sam has to get his, you know.'

"They looked at me and said: 'Who's he?' "

Pinky of St. Paul: "A while ago, I had a young man in my kitchen. He was helping me with yard work, and we came in to warm up and have a cup of coffee. So I turned on the percolator, and he looked at it and said: 'What's that?' "

Marie of Roseville: "I felt kind of old when my daughter handed me a Christmas list of things she wanted—done on the computer."

Pat of St. Paul: "My husband, son and I were . . . in the soda aisle, and my son wanted some 'Coke in a jar.' We finally figured out he meant the old bottles that Coke recently reintroduced. We came home, and he wanted to have his Coke in a jar and couldn't get the top off—so we also had to show him what a bottle opener was. It was kind of . . . strange."

A Bulletin Board Nut: "About four years ago, our family and another took our daughter and their son, both about 7, to the history museum in St. Paul, and at one point, they both turned to me and asked what was in this glass case.

132

"I looked over, and I said: 'You don't know what that is?' And they said: 'No. We have no idea what that is.' I couldn't keep from laughing, because I couldn't believe they had never seen anything like this in their whole life.

"I knew I was old when I looked in the case and saw a push lawn mower, without a motor on it. They had no idea what it was!"

Tim H. of St. Paul: "I was in the video-rental store with the girlfriend of a friend of mine, a couple of years ago. She was 19. We were trying to decide which movie to rent. Finally, she pipes up and says: 'Let's see an old movie—like *Star Wars*.'"

Cindy of St. Paul: "My 5½-year-old daughter is now referring to 'The Brady Bunch' as a show from 'the olden days.'"

The Mad Mother of Six Boys of Vadnais Heights: "I just found something that really makes me feel old. This is the first time in 25 years that we're coming up to Christmas—and nobody believes in Santa Claus in our house. It's really sad—but then again, I always believe in Santa Claus, and no matter what they tell me, I won't let those boys convince me there isn't a Santa Claus."

Nancy of St. Paul: "The other day, my 5-year-old daughter was explaining to her little friend what breasts were. She turned and said: 'Yeah, you know, those things that moms have in front that hang down.'

"I guess 'young and perky' is long gone."

Virginia of St. Paul: "After four children, I realized—when I was trying on a party dress—that a push-up bra actually has a very practical purpose. And does that ever make you feel old!

"I then had to go to the store and *buy* one, and I felt like I did in high school when I had to buy a box of tampons in front of anybody. I handed the bra over the counter, and I felt like she was thinking: 'Well, it's about time, lady.'"

Navasanki of St. Paul: "I got my first . . . gray . . . hair. I found it sitting right where I part my hair, of course, plain to the world, in neon, glowing silver-white. It's . . . over."

Sue of Woodbury: "Old is not finding your first gray hair; it's realizing that if you don't stop pulling out your gray hairs, you're gonna be bald."

Dave of Backus: "I realized I'd lost my youth when my washboard stomach started to turn into a washtub stomach."

Another John of St. Paul: "While I'm losing the hair on the top of my head, the hair in my ears and my nose is growing like wildfire. Can't quite figure that one out, but I guess it happens to all of us old guys."

Ted of North St. Paul: "My son is talking about dinosaurs—and he's getting old enough now that he knows more about dinosaurs than I do."

Judy of St. Paul Park: "I saw my son's name and 'For A Good Time' on a bathroom wall in a bar."

Gary R. of Fridley: "I was down in Chicago, in a lounge—sittin' there doin' my favorite thing, talkin' baseball. Another person sittin' there was in his early 20s, and I talked about how up in Minnesota, at the old Met, I used to see Harmon Killebrew and Rocky Colavito and Tony Oliva.

"His eyes bugged out, and he looked at me and said: 'You saw those guys *actually play?*' "

Ed of Inver Grove Heights: "I sell real estate. I'm working with two different buyers who were born in '73. I mean, these are post-Watergate babies! They're buying houses!

"When my 15-year-old first drove a car, I remember looking across at him and thinking: 'I'm not getting old.' But when I'm talking with somebody who doesn't remember Senator Ervin . . . that made me feel old."

Jilrin of Roseville: "For the first time, today I knew that I wasn't getting any younger.

"I was trying to read (hard to do in a house with teenagers) the morning paper; today the front section caught my attention first, and I slowly flipped through the news. As I got to the end of the section, there was a picture of an unnamed American soldier being dragged through the streets of Somalia by a rope tied to his hands.

"I grew up seeing the pictures of Vietnam, listing the names of those who wouldn't come home, wearing a bracelet with the name of a man I didn't know who never came home, seeing a family torn apart by a son who made the choice to go to Canada, and today as I tried to explain to my children why that picture brings back such vivid, painful memories of another time, I realized I must be old. I sure felt old."

Jan of Maplewood: "I always scan the obituaries. I look at last names and ages. And I realized I was really getting old when, instead of looking for the *parents* of my friends, I was looking to see if any of my *friends* had died."

Joan of Hudson, Wis.: "My daughter read me my horoscope this morning. It said: 'Check in on an older relative.' I stopped to think of who was older than I, and alas, there was no one. I'm the oldest."

Spiff of St. Paul: "In the mail on Tuesday, I received the current issues of *Spy* and *The Nation*. I read *The Nation* first."

Mom of Woodbury: "I used to get *Ms.*; then, I changed to *Redbook*; now, at age 36, I read *Good Housekeeping*."

C.J. of White Bear Lake: "I don't know if this is a sign of getting old, or maturity, but I'm watching Saturday-morning TV—and I kinda find Martha Stewart kinda hot."

Somebody's Dad of St. Paul: "My awakening came several months ago, when I was eating Oreos with my son—and realized that I like the chocolate wafers better than the creamy filling."

The Snackmeister of St. Paul: "I actually prefer eating Oreos with all of the layers still intact."

An Over-the-hill 30-year-old of Oakdale: "This weekend, it took me until I was pouring out the last bowl of Cap'n Crunch to realize that there was a prize inside. That's pretty sad. I used to buy that stuff just *for* the prize; now I don't even notice when there's one in there."

The Pathfinder of Shoreview: "*That's* not old; *I'm* old: I still think of Cap'n Crunch as a new cereal."

Carol of Roseville: "I realized I was getting old when one of the grocery-store bag boys called me 'Ma'am.' "

Nancy of Lakeville: "The kids left the bathroom light on, both of their bedroom lights on, and the hall light on, and I heard myself shouting from the kitchen: 'Hey, turn those lights off! What do you think—I own the Edison?'

"And I thought: 'Oh, my gosh. I've turned into my *mother.*' "

M.J.B. of the East Side: "When I went underwear shopping this past week-end, I bypassed the sexy, frilly bikinis (with matching bras, even!) and went straight to the four-packs of solid-colored, 100-percent-cotton briefs."

Donna of Afton: "I'm in the process of packing for a trip, and I noticed that I was not packing either tennis shoes or blue jeans."

Missy the Bartender of Mahtomedi: "My two sisters and I were up north this past summer, and we stopped at a bar. My two sisters are older than I am.

"We went and got a corner booth, and then I walked to the bar and or-dered the three drinks. The bartender said: 'Could I see your I.D., please?' I'm 29, and I haven't had my I.D. checked in a while, so I got all excited and did this little dance back to the table. And I went [in that naa-naa-na-naa-naa tone]: 'He wants to see my I.D.!'

"I went back to the bar, and the bartender was down at the other end, and then he came walking back, and he had all three drinks. I went: 'Well, here's my I.D.' And he said: 'Well, Ma'am, when you react like that, I don't have to see it anymore.' "

Jeanie of Woodbury: "I was a very young 42 when I had my first grand-child. Whenever I mentioned her, people would respond with: 'Oh, *you* don't look old enough to be a grandmother.' It made me feel so good. Well, it was a few years later when I met someone for the first time and their first question was: 'And how many grandchildren do you have?' "

Zing of North St. Paul: "I went to pick up my grandson tonight at religion class. And as I walk into the building, some little first-grade girl pipes up: 'Oh, here's somebody's grandfather.'

"I *am* 72, but I'd really hoped it wouldn't be quite so obvious."

Dusty Throat of North St. Paul, on behalf of herself and **The Big Woman:** "Last winter, while checking into a motel in Blackwell, Oklahoma, we asked the clerk if we could have the AARP discount. She looked at us and said: 'I've already given it to you.' Time to put away the bobby sox and the penny loafers."

Debbie of Stacy: "I just got home from work and opened up the mail—and I got a letter from Colonial Penn Insurance Company telling me they're gonna insure me as an 'older driver.' I'm de-*pressed!*"

Louise of St. Paul: "I had to fill out a form this week. The last question was the age bracket—like 18–29, 30–45 and so on. When I saw mine, 64 and a blank, I thought: 'Oh, no. I'm at the end of the line.' "

Gram of parts undisclosed: "I'm over 70 years old. My husband and I went to church Sunday morning, and every time we bowed our heads, our noses ran—and I think that's when we discovered: Hey, we're really over the hill."

P.J. of St. Paul: "The other day, I was standing in a copy store, sending a fax. They have a little newsstand there, and I picked up a copy of *Mad* magazine. Hadn't seen one since I was a kid. I flipped through it, and they had one of their little stories about '30 Years Ago Today'—about what happens during the first day of school. And for the first time, I realized that I wasn't the 'Today'; I was the '30 Years Ago.' "

Your Sweetheart of Forest Lake: "I just heard a commercial that brought to my attention my waning youth.

"When I read the book *1984*, that year was possible in my future. When I saw the movie *2001*, that year was in my future. But I just heard a commercial for *Demolition Man* about the year 2032, and I realized: That's really *not* possible in my future."

Terry B. of St. Paul Park: "This fall, I went to the nursery to look at trees. There was a pin oak that I really liked. I asked the young salesman how long it would be before it was a good-sized tree. He looked at me and said: 'Well, let me put it this way: You'll never see it happen.' "

Mother of 6 of Hastings: "My mom works at a retirement center and was talking to one of the guys there, and he said that he knew he was getting . . . so old that he didn't dare buy green bananas anymore."

Popo of White Bear Lake: "I tried to walk across my gravel-rocked driveway, and what I was saying was: 'Jesus! Mother! Oh my Lord! Help me, Mother Mary!'

"It made me think: As a child, you could practically crawl . . . you could inch your way across miles of a gravel driveway and not wince once. Ah, to be young again!"

The Other Ron of St. Paul: "I just got an idea how you can tell how old somebody is; it's a direct barometer: The more you say, 'I wish it were like the good old days,' the older you are.

"Very simple. Short. Sweet."

Sister of the Twins: "I play the flute in the most advanced flute section in my band, and a few days ago, our flute section was helping out the new flute players who've never played before. And our director, Mr. D————, was helping us, and all of these little fourth-graders . . . by the way, I'm in seventh grade . . . they were so excited over their new flutes, and that sort of led us into déjà vu. It took me back to when I was in fourth grade.

"Mr. D———— was explaining to them how to put their flutes together, and then he said to them: 'And if you can't get it, the big kids will help you.'

"And it just hit me: I'm a big kid! It doesn't make any sense, but I'm a big kid now!

"I remember . . . well, of course I remember, but I feel like I'm still down in the fourth-grade rooms, but . . . I'm a big kid now! That kinda made my day—not really made my day, but it made me see how much I've been growing lately.

"Stupid call-in—but I hope you print it. Bye."

BULLETIN BOARD REPLIES: Stupid? Not at all.

In fact, dear Sister of the Twins, we urge you to store this passage someplace cool, dry and secure. In about 30 years, dig it out—and see if you don't feel then just exactly as you feel now.

It's a strange thing, this growing older. Very strange.

You never catch up with yourself—as **LaVonne** *of Coon Rapids can attest:*

"I thought I was all grown-up 28 years ago, when a high-school principal, who only a year earlier would have scolded me for truancy, treated me like an equal and called me Mrs. Bucklen. (That's not my name anymore.)

"A few months later, when I heard a nurse calling 'Mrs. Bucklen! Mrs. Bucklen!' through my anesthetized haze, I wondered who she was talking about. I opened my eyes to find out, and she showed me my brand-new son, who just got married a few weeks ago. I don't feel grown-up enough for that at all."

CHAPTER 18

At the Intersection of Life and Death

*S*omewhere *between heaven and Earth:*

Jean of Roseville: "My mother-in-law passed away in the early '70s of a heart condition. She was very young; she was still in her 40s. She left behind two young teenagers at home, and she lived to see only two of her eventual nine grandchildren. They were just wee ones at the time.

"It was about five years later, and a bunch of the family was sitting around, talking and sharing stories about Grandma. The kids were there, and they were listenin', and everybody was laughing and getting, you know, kinda misty-eyed. We were sharing; it was really a good time.

"And my second son, who had not even been conceived when she died— he was about 4 at the time—piped up and said: 'I . . . I 'member Grandma.'

"And everybody said: 'No. No, sweetie. You don't remember Grandma. She died before you were born.'

"And he said: 'I 'member Grandma!'

"And everybody just kinda laughed at him and said: 'No, no. Isn't he cute?'—and kind of ignored him. And about a minute later, he got very upset, like a 4-year-old, and he said: 'I do too 'member Grandma. When I was in heaven waiting to be born, I knew Grandma.'

"Well, he just stunned this roomful of adults into silence; nobody knew what to say. My poor father-in-law was just so shaken for the rest of the day; it just really blew him away. It still makes the little hairs on my arms stand up right now to tell you this story, almost 20 years later. And this came from a kid who . . . at the time, we were not attending church; he had had absolutely no religious training. We had Santa and all of that, but we didn't take them to Sunday school.

"We still talk about that story. He's a special kid, and sometimes it makes you wonder if maybe she had not touched him in some way."

Pained of Lakeland: "My grandma Lena was a sweet, charming lady who left paper trails everywhere. By that, I mean: She would keep tissues and hankies up her sleeves rather than in her pockets, and they would invariably end up on the floor—at home, in restaurants, in shops, everywhere. It was one of her endearing eccentricities that always made us, her family, chuckle.

"In April 1982, she succumbed to the most cruel, merciless abdominal cancer. I found myself at her graveside services—conducted in a pretty little cemetery in Sebeka, Minnesota, a small town way up north—with about 30 Kleenexes in my hand, and while the preacher was talking about Grandma's contributions to her world, a sudden gust of wind tore those tissues out of my hand and carried them to the four corners of the Earth. They flew every which way—to the skies, to the trees. Some even flew into that awful, gaping hole where my beloved grandma would soon be laid.

"Through my tears, I laughed—because I knew that Grandma caused this. In death as in life, she wanted no one to suffer—especially on her own behalf.

"What someone said of Audrey Hepburn is definitely applicable to my angelic grandma: A silver bell has been silenced."

JoAnn B. of West St. Paul: "Many years ago, my father suffered a serious stroke, and I didn't know if he would survive—or if he did, what the quality of his life would be.

"I knew he was on the road to recovery when his doctor said to him: 'You're just going to have to stop smoking, drinking and lose that extra weight—or you can write me off as your doctor.'

"My father's response was: 'Well, who would you recommend?'

"He accomplished only one out of three of the doctor's orders, but I was blessed with an additional 10 years of his humor and love before an unrelated illness took him home.

"A few hours before he died, I told him he was going to be a grandfather again. Seven months later, my beautiful son was born and looked remarkably like his 'Papa,' right down to the bald head.

"Six years has not dimmed my belief that a guardian angel was watching over me during my father's decline, and I was given the gift of life in the face of death."

Amy of St. Paul: "A few years ago, my stepfather got cancer and died. He and my mother lived near Ellsworth, Wisconsin, in a real lovely country home. A couple weeks after the funeral, my young son came home from the grocery with a helium balloon. He said: 'I miss Grandpa, and I want to send him a message and see what heaven is like.' Then he said: 'Mom, can you help me write my name and address, so he knows it's me trying to get ahold of him?'

"So we wrote his name and address, and we put it in a baggie, and we tied it on the helium balloon. We lived in Highland at the time; he went out and let it loose in a field in Highland. And that was the end of it. About five days later, I got a phone call—and it was from a man in Ellsworth, Wisconsin, who was the man who cut firewood and shoveled the walk for my mother and her husband.

"He said: 'Are you Vi's daughter?' And I said: 'Yes.' And he gave his name, and he said: 'I was out clearing brush from the fence line and chopping firewood, and I found a balloon that was hooked on the bushes.' And he said: 'I went over and looked at it, and there was something hanging on it, and it was your phone number. And I thought: "My God, that's Vi's daughter's last name." '

"So he called, and it was on the property line of my stepfather's place. That's where this balloon had traveled—from St. Paul to Ellsworth, Wisconsin. I was just astounded, and I told my young son. I said: 'Jess, your balloon went to Grandpa's property. They found your balloon on Grandpa's property.' And he said: 'Oh, good, Grandpa got my message!'

"That still just moves me incredibly. I can't believe that this could ever have taken place. That's one for the books, I guess."

R.J. of Hammond, Wis.: "My dad was editor and publisher of a small-town weekly newspaper right up until he had a stroke, just after his 88th birthday. In fact, he wouldn't even go to the hospital until his paper had gone to press.

"He was pretty remarkable—and he was eccentric, too. He always thought rules didn't apply to him; if a sign said 'Keep Out,' he never thought that that meant him. Maybe that was the newspaperman in him? He was also the ultimate pack rat: He saved everything—especially newspapers, rubber bands, paper napkins from restaurants. He loved flowers, and our yard had all kinds of wildflowers, all colors of violets. His favorite of all was the blue violet.

"About a year and a half after his stroke, he died. It was three years ago, the night before Father's Day.

"The next spring, I bought three violets at a church sale—a white-and-blue one, a reddish-purple one and a blue one—intending to plant them on Dad's grave in Michigan. But I never got to Michigan before cold weather, so I just stuck 'em in my flower bed and figured I could divide each clump into three parts the next spring—one for the cemetery, one for my sister and one for me.

"Last year, they all came up, but when the white and the red ones bloomed, the blue one had disappeared completely. It even looked like it had been pulled up from the ground. No one but me ever goes to the flower bed, so it just didn't make sense.

"Meantime, my sister visited the cemetery, and there were blue violets all over Dad's grave—and nowhere else nearby at all. All his other friends and family are dead, so no one but her ever goes there. As she was leaving, in the drive beside the grave, somebody had dumped a bunch of restaurant napkins and rubber bands all over. She just had to laugh, because it was as if he had been there.

"At home the next day, her daughter brought her a bouquet of blue violets, and she said: 'Where did you get those? We don't have any in our yard.' Her daughter said: 'Yes, we do. They're all over the yard.' And so they were.

"Later, just before Father's Day, I was working out in the yard, and it dawned on me that it was about two years to the hour since Dad had died. I was feeling pretty sad, and I happened to walk over to the violets—and that blue violet was back, in the exact spot where it had not been even three days before. It just was so odd to find it at that particular moment.

"And this spring, there's violets everywhere in my fields and woods—thousands of 'em. And I just had to chuckle, because it would be so like Dad to get impatient waiting for me to divvy up the plants, and to find a way to comfort me—and if heaven has any rule about not going back to Earth, he would be trying to find a way to thwart it.

"Dad, if you can get your hands on a newspaper up there, I know you're reading this. Happy Father's Day."

Lou of North St. Paul: "I have a granddaughter who's almost 4 years old now. She lost her grandmother a year and a half ago, and now, every time she sees a rainbow, she tells her mother that that's Grandma, painting the sky for her."

Mo of Minneapolis: "In the early '80s, I lived with my family in a western city known for its beautiful mountain ranges. We were lucky enough to find a home in the foothills overlooking the valley, and when it rained we were treated to some of the most spectacular rainbows I've ever seen.

"Shortly after we moved there, we discovered we were expecting our second child. I decided to really go all out this time and decorate the nursery in rainbows—wallpaper, curtains, quilts, everything. This upstairs room faced the valley, with hills sloping upward on both sides.

"On the day that my friend 'Mary' finished the wallpaper, it had rained in the morning. We were sitting in the nursery admiring her wonderful work, and suddenly the sun came out and there were rainbows everywhere! I took it as a sign from the Lord that everything was going to be fine.

"It was not to be. Shortly after our second son was born, prematurely, he died of infection, in spite of the excellent care at one of the best children's hospitals in the country. On the day we buried him, my husband and I each saw rainbows from different parts of the city. To me it seemed so sad. Afterward, I went home and closed the door forever on that room.

"It has taken many years of recovery from that grief, and his father and I are divorced, but I have made a beautiful new life for myself and found my way back to my faith. Today when I see a rainbow, especially around his birthday, I take it as a big 'Hi, Mommy!' from my 10-year-old angel, and I always wave back."

Lynne of Bloomington: "I had a little mutt-type dog—a terrier mix named Squeaker; Squeaker McGee—for 14½ years. He came into my life on October 1, 1971. People often said he looked kind of like Toto.

"In December of 1985, he developed kidney failure—rapidly, and despite all treatment, irreversibly. Finally, my vet told me that to continue treatment would be futile and that within four to six days, Squeaker would begin to be really ill, and I would have to stop his pain permanently.

"He started feeling bad on a Saturday eve; on Sunday morning, I got my vet to go into the clinic to put him to sleep. Anyone who has had to make this decision with a beloved pet knows how hard it is. After all, when I was in the depths of horrible depression, my therapist knew that as long as I had him to care for and because he depended on *me*, I wouldn't be able to end my life.

"Sunday morning was awful. I listen to the big-band radio station, and I never turn off the radio when I turn off the car. So when we got in the car and I started it up, the radio was on immediately—and the very first thing I heard was Judy Garland saying, 'There's got to be a place, Toto, somewhere far, far away' and then the song 'Over the Rainbow.'

"I had known, logically, that I was doing the best for my dog; hearing 'Over the Rainbow' not only gave me goose bumps, but it also was an incredible affirmation that I was doing the right thing.

"If there's a heaven, and I make it there, my little dog will be there. Otherwise, it won't be heaven."

CHAPTER 19

"A Little Song, A Little Dance, A Little Seltzer Down Your Pants"

*T*hat, *of course, was the motto of the late, great Chuckles the Clown (of the late, great "Mary Tyler Moore Show"), whose funeral kept coming to mind as we heard these stories of totally inappropriate—but usually unsquelchable— laughter:*

Chris of St. Paul: "When we were young, my mother used to give us all haircuts, and she wasn't the most proficient hair-cutter in the world—so we'd frequently come out with clumps gone here and clumps gone there.

"About 10 years ago, as my dad was dying of leukemia, he was out of the hospital just long enough to attend the funeral of my grandfather. We were all sitting in the memorial chapel, saying our good-byes to my grandfather, when the mortician came in—a well-known mortician who . . . he has a lot of bad hair days, let's just say.

"He walked in the room, and my father—who was only months away from his own funeral—leaned over to all of us and, without a trace of a smile, said: 'It looks like your mother's back cutting hair again.'

"Needless to say, it was difficult to sit through the rest of the service with the mortician up in front."

Jeanette of Siren, Wis.: "This happened back in the mid-'60s, when my younger brother was graduating from high school. I was already married by that time; I was a wife and mother, and I had my life in order.

"Well, before the commencement exercises, he had spent *hours* combing his hair. He wanted to get it just right; he had used wave set (if you can remember that) and was just doing everything to get that long hair in place. And then I told him how egg white works really good, so he was using egg white on his hair, and by the time he walked out the door, his hair looked great.

"Well, the commencement exercises started, and all the seniors marched in, and he looked so nice in his cap and gown—but then they opened with a prayer and the National Anthem. Of course, the guys all removed their caps—and there stands my brother with his hair absolutely *plastered* to his head. All of this gook that he had put on had just smashed his hair down.

"Well, it broke me up, and I started to giggle. Of course, he glanced over at me, and he was trying to keep a straight face, and he's breaking up. The harder I tried to stop laughing, the more uncontrollable were the giggles. My mother is sitting next to me, and *she* starts giggling, just because it's contagious. My father has no idea what is going on; he keeps looking at us, helplessly, and glaring at us. And it's very embarrassing—mainly because my father is a pastor in this town, and here he has his whole family broke up and giggling during the National Anthem."

Bernadette of Coon Rapids: "I have something cute to tell about my son, whose grandfather died about two weeks ago. While attending the funeral, my 5-year-old was very concerned about his grandfather being in the box. And I explained to him that only grandpa's body was in the box, and his soul and spirit were all around us. And he looked up at my husband and me with his big brown eyes, and he said, 'What did they do with his head?'

"It broke us up at a very sad time and made us realize that life is for living."

Judy E. of Apple Valley: "At a funeral several years ago for an elderly lady who had died, my niece was with her mother, walking up to look at the person in the casket, and there were two other elderly women there, saying, 'Oh, she looks like she's just asleep. She looks so natural.'

"And the little 4-year-old went up and stuck her head over the side of the coffin and said: 'She looks dead to me.' Just brought the house down."

Alan Schroeder of Chester, Iowa, reporting on his uncle's funeral Mass: "At one point during the service, they rang a small set of bells. They must have stolen them off a Good Humor truck, because they sounded just like them.

"My brother and I started to laugh to ourselves so hard that our parents later said we were shaking the pew. Every time they rang these bells, it got worse. Even my parents started laughing. None of us would look at each other, because if we had, we would have started rolling in the aisles.

"As we left the church, my father leaned over and said: 'Chocolate or vanilla?' This time, we couldn't help ourselves.

"I think some of our family must still wonder what we thought was so funny outside of the church for Uncle John's funeral."

Ol' Virginny of Cottage Grove: "My daughter, who lives in Tucson, went to the last rites of her girlfriend's husband, who was killed in a tragic motorcycle accident. According to his wishes, his ashes were to be strewn in a very scenic place on his favorite mountain at the top of a pass.

"Everything was going along just fine until a sudden brisk breeze blew the ashes to the widow and my daughter, and they inhaled some of the dust and started sneezing fits. My daughter said, as the dust went up her nose: 'Gee, I feel closer to him now than I did when he was alive'—and they broke into hysterical giggles, which didn't stop until they turned into tears.

"It was kind of hard to explain to the rest of the mourners, who had been giving them some dirty looks."

Anonymous woman of St. Paul: "Several years ago, I had the misfortune to have to attend a funeral for a very wonderful woman who'd died very unexpectedly. The church was full to its capacity with people who had come to pay their respects. It was at a time when the song 'Wind Beneath My Wings' was very, very popular, and it had been selected as a song to be played during the funeral—right after the oldest grandson had delivered a eulogy he was unable to finish because he was so choked up.

"Well, the time for the music came, and whoever was operating the record player dropped the needle on the wrong spot. The church was filled with 'Under the Boardwalk.' People had been crying so hard before, during the eulogy, that it went immediately to tears of laughter. You could see people's shoulders quivering because they couldn't help but laugh. Nobody dared look at each other, because it would have gotten even worse."

Susan of Burnsville: "A year ago, I was at the funeral of my best friend and her husband, who were tragically killed. A lot of my family came for the double funeral, and my father was asked to perform the service. After he spoke, a singer played and sang 'Wind Beneath My Wings' on one of those hokey, cheap-sounding funeral-home organs. Since he was playing for himself, he had to keep pausing in the middle of a phrase to turn the page himself, and he neither played nor sang very well. 'I can fly higher than aaaaaaaaaan . . . (pause, flip) . . . eagle.' All the tension of the past few days escaped in a fit of uncontrollable giggling, and my mother, who was sitting next to me, started giggling, too. She was poking me in the side to make me stop, and we both had to hang our heads down, hoping everyone would think we were extremely moved. She and I agreed later that it made the service bearable, and that my friends would understand, because they were probably laughing, too.

"Thanks for letting me confess."

Beth of White Bear Lake: "Last year, we went to my husband's elderly aunt's funeral. She was a Benedictine nun, and she lived a long, productive life. We went to her funeral over in Eau Claire, and the nuns there were so sweet; they treated us like royalty.

"The kids were very interested in seeing this poor, dead nun; I mean, they had never seen a dead body before. We had tried to explain, as best we could, all about death. And we went to the cemetery, and they were burying her, and they passed around the little holy-water thing that you sprinkle onto the coffin.

"My 7-year-old kept saying: 'Mom, what are they doing? Mom, what are they doing?'

"I said: 'Shhh, shhh. We'll tell you later. We'll tell you later.' But he kept insisting that he wanted to know why everyone was sprinkling this water. You know, we were standing there with all these nuns practically on top of us, listening to every word we were saying.

"Finally, he blurted out, after about the 50th nun sprinkled holy water on the casket: 'Oh, is that so she doesn't rot?'

"I just was mortified. I was so embarrassed—until I turned around and saw all these old nuns stifling their laughter. They thought it was hilarious."

Gary of Woodbury: "When I was 12 years old or so—that was about 30 years ago—I was an altar boy. It used to be a real good deal to get a funeral, because it paid a few bucks, back then, from the family of the person who'd died.

"We had this old monsignor doing the funeral Mass, and it turned out he had a little trouble with gas. So at one of the funerals that I was doing, he had, shall I say, rather audible flatulence.

"It started off right away. The other altar boy and I started to break out in laughter every time this monsignor would let a few fly, and we just couldn't stop. Absolutely could not stop. He kept muttering 'Shut up! Shut up!' under his breath. And about halfway through, we had to go down and bless the casket—and I knew that was comin', and the other guy knew that was comin', and the more I thought about it, the harder I laughed."

"A Little Song, A Little Dance, A Little Seltzer Down Your Pants"

Laure of the West Side: "In 1986, my Uncle George passed away. Uncle George was a really funny guy whom you could always count on to stir things up at family gatherings. He loved to tease.

"Well, I went to the church for his funeral and saw my family sittin' near the front, so I went and sat with them. The service was really nice, and when Uncle George's son gave the eulogy, I cried. Uncle George was always a favorite of mine, and it hit me then how strange it would be without him.

"I wiped my nose and eyes and took a deep breath as the immediate family started to file out of the pews in front of us. The ushers stepped up to the pew in front of us, and we proceeded to follow the others out. As I looked at various people on the way down the aisle, some averted their gaze, and others smiled at me.

"When we got outside, I said to my sister Sue: 'People were *smilin'* at me on the way out. Isn't that weird?'

"She looked at me, and she said: 'That's prob'ly because you've got a big white booger on the end of your nose.'

"God, did we laugh—and at the luncheon afterwards, I couldn't help but feel a little disappointed that no one teased me about it. Uncle George would have."

Bob of Little Canada, sounding awfully like Tom Bodet: "About 20 years ago, I worked at an orchard in southwestern Wisconsin with a man named Waldo. Waldo was in his 70s; he was kinda hunchbacked, and semicrippled with arthritis.

"We were riding on the front of a trailer that was being pulled behind a tractor and a sprayer. When we started down over a hillside, the man on the tractor lost control—and the tractor started sliding. I saw what was gonna happen, and I jumped to safety—but Waldo did not.

"When the sprayer rolled over, it lifted the front of the trailer several feet up into the air, which threw Waldo up into the air. He came down in the middle of the trailer, bounced back up in the air, came down on the rear end of the trailer just as *that* was comin' back up, and that batted him several feet back up into the air, and he finally landed behind the trailer.

"I was sure he was dead—or at least had multiple compound fractures and internal injuries. I was very concerned—but the sight of him bouncin' across that trailer like a stone skippin' across a pond, was kinda like something out of a Buster Keaton movie, and when I walked over to check him out, I just had to turn away—'cause I was in tears from tryin' not to break up.

"Beyond some bruises, Waldo was unhurt."

147

Sally of White Bear Lake: "My father was a very healthy 76-year-old who had helped a neighbor move farm equipment just before they were both killed in an automobile accident.

"My dad had been an active member of the Masonic Lodge all of his life, so the Masons in the small rural community where I grew up held a traditional prayer service for the family at the funeral home.

"Apparently, there aren't many new members in the Masonic Lodge, because all of the men who participated in my dad's service were quite elderly. As we watched the line of Masons march in, wearing the traditional leather aprons, we could see that almost all of them needed the assistance of canes or metal walkers. This came as quite a shock to me, since my dad had been so active.

"I whispered to my brother-in-law: 'My God! They're in worse shape than my dad!' We immediately got the giggles, and as we sat there with our heads down and our shoulders shaking, my mother leaned over and said to us: 'You two, cut it out!'

"Both my brother-in-law and I were 40 years old at the time."

R.D.K. of Wisconsin: "Great Uncle Mike died; had a Mason's funeral, with his lodge brothers doing a ritual called something like 'boosting their brother to the heavens,' in which, wearing these little white aprons, they marched around and around the coffin and, with arms upraised, pointed their thumbs skyward and tossed palm fronds into the open casket—one of which stuck in Great Uncle's nostril.

"My father and I began to laugh, snorting and biting our gloves, trying to contain ourselves. My mother was absolutely outraged at our behavior, and the more she prodded us and glared at us, the worse we got.

"When we finally got under control (unfortunately, as we were walking out), my nearly deaf grandfather asked my dad, 'Say, who was that up front who was crying so over Mike?'—which, of course, sent us off again.

"My mother still rags on us about what jerks we were, and this happened at least 30 years ago. It still sends me off into near-hysteria. The best thing was that Mike would have laughed right with us."

Amy of St. Paul: "My younger sister, Erin, was in a car accident a few years ago, and they rushed her to this Catholic hospital. We're not Catholic; we're Lutheran—but they didn't seem to mind.

"My mother and I were sitting there, and we had all been at the hospital for three or four days, and hadn't slept at all, and hadn't eaten much, and hadn't showered, and we were just really tired and depressed. Well, there was this priest who was really pompous, like priests sometimes can be, and he was struttin' around the hospital, and he was just Mr. Friendly, always sayin' 'How ya doin'?' and wavin' to people—and it was just drivin' us nuts.

"And one day, my mom and I decided to go out and sit in one of the open waiting rooms right by the elevator, and they have these big pillars outside of the elevator. And this priest, of course, comes walkin' by and sees us, and he's wavin' and sayin' hi to us—and he walks straight into one of the poles. It was the funniest thing I ever saw."

Gina of St. Paul: "A few years ago, my mother was in a terrible car accident in Milwaukee, suffered a severe brain injury, and was in a coma for three weeks. She was placed in the neurological intensive-care unit at a big, brand-new hospital. The unit had about 15 beds, and each of them was occupied by a patient who was either at or near brain death.

"The waiting room, which was a really terrible place, was a really small space where family members filled in the time between hourly five-minute visits with their unconscious loved one. It was in this place that families were shown CAT scans and given graphic descriptions of the patients' condition. It was also the place where the transplant surgeons met with family members of still-living patients to request permission to harvest any usable organs after life support was turned off.

"Directly across the hall from this room was a door marked, simply, 'Proctoscope Room.' I'm not kidding. During one particularly grueling day in the waiting room, we saw this little elderly man wearing a hospital gown and being led into this room by a very determined-looking nurse. A few minutes later, we heard this yelping and moaning coming from the room; it was really terrible. It went on and on—or maybe it just seemed to. We all looked at each other and just broke into hysterical laughter. And it was really bad, because the louder the moaning got, the louder we laughed. Anyway, when the door opened, we all shut up really fast, and the old man was led away, and he really looked like he had been through something—which, I guess, he had. He sorta glanced into our waiting room, and I'm sure he had no idea that he had provided us with a few desperately needed moments of merriment during a heartbreaking time.

"After it was all over, we talked about how really stupid it was to put a proctoscope room in that place—but now when I look back on it, I think maybe some hospital planner had a good sense of humor."

Anita of St. Paul: "I was a very lowly nurse's aide in a hospital in South Dakota, and we had this very, very elegant doctor who used to find ways to put lowly nurse's aides in their place.

"This one day when I was working in the nursery, he came in and said: 'May I see Baby W's circumcision?' And I said: 'Certainly.' So with my best nurse's aide training, I undiapered Baby W and exposed him to this elegant doctor—and Baby W did a good job for me. He peed all the way down this elegant doctor's face, white shirt and tie.

"I could hardly wait for this elegant doctor to leave, and then I sat on the floor and rolled around and laughed."

Deb of Roseville: "My father was in the hospital. We didn't realize it, but he was dying. He had had both of his legs amputated; he was a diabetic. We'd gone through a lot of stressful times over the two weeks previous to the amputations, and when the doctor was going to take us in to see our dad, they warned us that we would not be seeing the lower portions of his legs or his feet. They were going to leave one of his legs longer, so they could fit him with a prosthesis. So we were anticipating what we would see when we walked into the room.

"We were not, however, anticipating the reply we got from the doctor when we asked what the name of his nurse was for the night. Her name was Eileen. Somehow or other, it just totally cracked my sister and me up. We had to immediately leave the room and head to the waiting room, where we proceeded to laugh ourselves into hysterics—and then eventually we bawled our eyes out."

CHAPTER 20

The Lowest Common Consumer

*H*elpful hints that really shouldn't be necessary:

Q.T. of the East Side: "I went into a men's room, and it smelled really good—like strawberry or something; I'd never smelled a bathroom that smelled that good. So I walk up to use the urinal, and I'm standing at the urinal doing what you do at urinals, and there was a sticker on the wall—it wasn't graffiti or handwriting; it was a *sticker*—and printed on it was: 'Please Do Not Eat the Urinal Cakes.'

"Now, I think if anybody is old enough to read, they know better than to eat the urinal cakes."

Elizabeth of Eagan: "My husband is getting ready to go deer hunting this weekend, and he has several bottles of attractant for deer. On the back is a warning; it says: 'DANGER. Do not apply to your body or clothing; you may be attacked. Not for human consumption. Do not intentionally ingest.'"

BULLETIN BOARD ADDS: And do not wear gag antlers.

Mary Shanley of Brooklyn Park: "My cousin had one of those baby walkers, and my aunt looked at the directions to see how to fold it up. At the very head of the directions, it says: 'Remove child.' I can just see these people, standing around, going: 'What the heck happened to the kid?' And another one going: 'Gee, I don't know. The last time I saw him, he was in his walker.' "

Nursing Nancy of Vadnais Heights: "Ellie, our round-faced, adorable 6-month-old, is teething, so I bought one of those water-filled plastic teething rings that you can put in the refrigerator. It's made by the baby-product com-

151

pany whose name has become an adjective to describe round-faced, adorable 6-month-olds.

"My husband and I noticed a warning on the package: 'Remember: Children are precious, and no product replaces adult supervision.' How stupid do they think parents of infants are? *[BULLETIN BOARD NOTES: However stupid that may be, Gerber (oops!) and its lawyers certainly must be in possession of whatever evidence of parental stupidity is available.]*

"We didn't exactly think the teething ring would be able to provide day care while we were at work—although I admit we were kinda hoping to put the ring in charge while we caught a movie and a quick bite to eat.

"My husband wants to ask it to water the plants and let the dog out. However, I feel this would be taking unfair advantage of the situation.

"I'm afraid we are really not going to get much use out of it. Anything that doesn't mind being chewed on by a grinning, drooling, nearly toothless mouth probably wouldn't make a very good supervisor, after all."

Dave's Gramma of Stillwater: "My new fat-free life includes products that seem like a real stretch to have ever been invented. The fat-free cream-cheese container says: 'This product is not a cure for heart disease.' Now there's a surprise."

Dave of Mendota Heights: "When I bought my son a Batman set for Christmas, the box had a warning on it: 'Cape does not allow user to fly.' Needless to say, we were very disappointed."

Joe of Inver Grove Heights: "I was recently cleaning my Bunn coffee maker, running vinegar through it, and I decided to check the owner's manual just to make sure I was doing it right.

"After letting the vinegar sit for a couple hours, the manual directed, I should 'pour 10 pitchers of fresh water into the top of the brewer' and—get this—'empty the decanter between pitchers.' Duuuhyeeeee."

Cheech of Burnsville: "I was putting together my answering machine, and when I was reading the instructions, I came to a part where it says 'Telephone Operation: To answer a call, lift the handset, converse, and when the call is over, hang up.'

"I'm glad they put that in there, because I wasn't sure if I should converse, then lift the handset and then hang up, or if I should pick up the phone, then hang up, then converse."

Sergeant Bilko of St. Paul: "Whilst hanging up to dry the nonskid rubber shower mat yesterday, I noticed that the suction-cup side said: 'This Side Down.' Uh-huh."

Anonymous woman of St. Paul: "My husband had a hot-air gun to melt the paint off the side of the house, and on the side of the box it said: 'Warning: Not intended for use as a hair dryer.' "

Cherie of Maplewood: "I just bought a new hair dryer, and under the warnings, it says: 'To reduce the risk of burns, electrocution, fire or injury to persons, never use while sleeping.' "

Theresa of St. Paul: "I have a sample-size box of Cheer laundry detergent, and it gives directions on the back: '1) Sort, select temperature, and begin filling washer with water. 2) See side panel for measuring/pouring instructions.' So then you see the side panel, and there—with illustrations, even—it says: '1) Remove top. 2) Pour contents into washer.' And then you return to the back to see what to do after that. It says: '3) Add clothes.' They devoted a whole lot of time and space to showing how to get the top off the box. I just wonder if there's anybody out there who'd just throw the box in there with the clothes. Might work; you never know."

Shirley of St. Paul: "I just bought a box that contains a set of kebab skewers, with a rack; the box is maybe eight inches by 10 inches. In little tiny print on the front of the box, it says: 'Gas Grill Not Included.' "

Red of Oakdale: "I just went to Rainbow Foods and bought this microwavable carameled-apple kit. Inside the box was a container of caramel and 10 Popsicle-type sticks. My 8-year-old pointed out these words on the box: 'Apples not included.' "

Bethany of St. Paul: "Today at lunch, while eating my fruit roll-up, I noticed the helpful instructions on the side. It says: 'Please peel fruit from cellophane before eating.' "

Mark of Brooklyn Center: "I was making Sloppy Joes the other night. We looked in the Betty Crocker cookbook, and it's kinda interesting. Here's how the recipe goes: one pound ground beef, one medium onion, blah-blah-blah, chopped celery, green bell pepper, ketchup, water, Worcestershire sauce, salt, red-pepper sauce, and six hamburger buns, split and toasted. It reads like this: 'Cook and stir ground beef and onion in 10-inch skillet until beef is brown. Drain. Stir in remaining ingredients, except buns. Cover and cook over low heat for 10 minutes.' Blahdity-blahdity-blah.

"I just thought that Betty Crocker takes me for granted a little bit here."

Cakemaker of St. Paul: "My sister and I were just looking at the Wilderness Classic Pumpkin Pie recipe that came along with a coupon. Buy two, get one free! The recipe reads: 'Preheat oven to 425 degrees. In large mixing bowl, combine all ingredients except pastry shell.' Duh.

"I'm glad I buy my pies frozen, already made."

Neal of St. Paul, open-eared while watching the local news: "They had a feature on vasectomies—how vasectomies could be linked to cancer. And they advised their viewing public to 'consult a physician before having a vasectomy.' As opposed to buying one of those self-vasectomy kits at the drugstore, I suppose."

Dave of Scandia, an open-eyed TV watcher: "They were honoring Martin Luther King and were showing some excerpts of one of his speeches—and in the middle of the speech, it came on the screen: 'Recorded earlier.' Duh."

Timbo of St. Paul: "I read to you from the side of a package that I purchased at a local department store this afternoon: 'WARNING: Do not use in situations where personal safety could be endangered. Misuse could result in serious injury or death.'

"Well, that's pretty straightforward. What is the product, you ask? It's twine—heavy-duty jute twine. I pity the poor soul who meets his death in a bizarre twine accident."

Seeker of St. Paul: "I was washing and drying the Kemps special holiday-decorated five-quart ice-cream pail that Ice Cream Man had just finished off when I noticed printed on the bottom: 'FREEZER SAFE.' Duh, right? Well, at our house, no pail of ice cream is safe."

Janet Llerandi of St. Paul, who always reads the instructions: "I have one of those cardboard sunshades for my car's window. It has detailed instructions in three steps—which, when condensed, just say, 'Put this in your windshield.'

"But step number four is the one that's really good. It's written in big, bold, red letters and it says, 'Warning: Do not drive with autoshade in place. Remove from windshield before starting ignition.' This thing really cracks me up every time I put it in the windshield."

Kathy of St. Paul: "My college-educated neighbor lady asked me how I drive my van with the cardboard sun screen in the window. See, those directions *are* for somebody."

CHAPTER 21

Dumb Customer Jokes

Fractional witticisms from all over:

Lynne Wunderlich of Bloomington: "For several years, I managed . . . a maternity and children's shop—and at the time, the Frederick's of Hollywood store was right next door. And all these people, all day long, would go by and point at the models in Frederick's and say 'Ha, ha, ha. First you go in there. . . .'—and then they'd point at us and say '. . . and then you'd go in *there!'* It got *real* old."

Will of St. Paul: "I'm an usher/ticket taker at a local sports arena. Occasionally, one of my assignments is to take tickets at the handicapped entrance. Right above the door, there's the universal handicapped symbol, clearly marked. Because that line is usually the shortest, people always come up—and I have to explain to them that they can't enter there.

"At that point, I'd say about 90 percent of the patrons give me a big smile and start limping away."

Ed of Eagan: "When we walked up to a restaurant and they said, 'Do you have reservations?', my dad would always say: 'Yes, but we're gonna eat here anyway.'"

The Flower Woman of St. Paul: "When I'm taking an order over the phone and I ask what credit card they'd like to use, people say 'Yours'—and they laugh hysterically."

Kirsten of St. Paul: "When waitressing, I would set down the check and say: 'You can pay me when you're ready.' They would invariably respond: 'OK. How 'bout next week?' I, in turn, would dutifully laugh; I wanted that tip."

Mrs. Foot (married to Mr. Foot—in mouth?) of Stillwater: "My husband probably drives waitresses crazy with his Dumb Customer Jokes. Whenever they ask how he wants his eggs done, he says: 'Cooked.' And when they bring

156

the bill for us to pay, he always tells them: 'Oh, we're not staying for the drawing.' "

Diane of Blaine: "When I was in college, I worked as a waitress. I would go up to a table of men and ask what they would like. And their reply would be: 'A waitress—with nothin' on it.' My reply would be: 'I just sold the last one 10 minutes ago.' "

Sarah of Maplewood, with a McDumb Customer Joke: "The Dumb Customer Joke I hate the most is: 'I thought this was *fast* food.' Or when they come up with an empty burger wrapper and say: 'Can I get a refill on this?' "

Bethie of St. Paul, anticipating a Dumb Job-seeker Joke: "Out on Robert Street, the Hardee's sign says: 'NOW HIRING FRESH FRIED CHICKEN.' It kinda makes me wonder: How many people have gone in there, introduced themselves as fresh fried chicken, and asked for a job?"

BULLETIN BOARD REPLIES: A more interesting question might be: How many of them got a job?

Kathy of St. Paul: "I own this leopard Appaloosa stallion—which means he's a white horse with large, multicolored spots all over his body that are about the size of your fist. Whenever I take him to shows, people say: 'Oh, that's a horse of a different color.' Or: 'Look at the big Dalmatian.' Ha, ha."

Sarah of Cumberland, Wis.: "I've been a waitress for five years now. We have a large, elaborate dessert tray—decorated with carrots that are carved to look like palm trees, with green peppers on top. It never fails; you go through the whole dessert tray, and someone will say: 'I'll have the carrot.' "

Eric of the Midway: "Where I work, we have a Dot Sale on. And it seems like every day, some funny jokester will walk in and say: 'So how much are the dots?' "

Dale of Fridley: "If you've ever put on a garage sale, inevitably someone will come up and say: 'So, how much are you selling the garage for?' "

Anonymous woman of St. Paul, a hotel coat checker: 'A Dumb Customer Joke that comes up all the time is: 'I'll take the fur.' I heard it last night about a hundred times."

Mike of Vadnais Heights: "I was selling lottery tickets last night, and every other person must've told me that they wanted a Powerball ticket—but only if it's the winner."

Jim of St. Paul: "My wife and I took a tour of the Winnipeg mint—where they make the Canadian coins. There were 12 of us on the tour, and 10 of them came up with the original line 'Do you give free samples?' We were the two who showed restraint."

Mary of Cottage Grove: "I work at a bank, and you'd be amazed at how many people come in on payday, want to cash a $25 check—and when we ask 'em how they'd like that back, they tell us they want it in hundreds."

Katie of West St. Paul: "I used to cashier, and when something wouldn't scan, customers would say: 'Oh! That one must be *free!*' "

Whales of Woodbury: "I was at Rainbow last night, and I heard probably the dumbest Dumb Customer Joke I've ever heard.

"The cash-register guy goes: 'Is everything current?' And the lady goes: 'Everything but my name and address.'

"She laughed."

Lucy of Dinkytown: "Last night, I heard the ultimate Dumb Customer Joke. I was in a convenience store in my neighborhood, and this guy walks up to the cashier and says: 'So, you come here often?' "

Cashier of parts undisclosed: "Anyone who has ever worked retail as a cashier knows that the stupidest customer joke of all is: Every time a customer owes you an even amount—like six bucks—they always say: 'Six bucks even? I bet that *never* happens! Ha-ha-ha-ha!'

"Well, it *always* happens! It happens *all the time!*"

Wendy of Barron, Wis.: "I went to Wal-Mart the other day and purchased three items. The total cost was $4 even. I kept my mouth shut and made no smart comment about it—and the *clerk* said: 'Four dollars, even. I'll bet you couldn't do that again if you tried!'"

BULLETIN BOARD MUSES: First day on the job, no doubt.

Joe Otte of St. Paul: "About 10 years ago, I was buying some parakeet seed—just a box of parakeet seed. I'm up in the checkout line, and the gal asks me if I want a bag for it, and I looked at her and said: 'No, I'll eat it here.' There was no response at all; she just looked at me."

Kathy of Cottage Grove: "I work at a drive-in movie theater in the summer. I'm a carhop—which means that when you drive up in your car, I'm the one who comes out with a big smile, says 'Hi,' takes your money, gives you your tickets, and sends you on your way.

"At our theater, the prices are different for adults and children—and children under 12 are admitted free. Well, these customers come up—I swear this happens hundreds of times a night—and I say: 'Hi. Would you like two adult tickets?' And *invariably*, one of them will just smile at me with this innocent smile and say: 'But I'm under 12.'

"They just laugh and laugh, like it's just the funniest thing they've ever heard! Makes me want to scream!"

Anonymous woman: "I work in payroll, and it seems that everyone who sees me or comes into my office during the day has to say: 'Put a little extra in my check this week!' Ha, ha, ha. Or: 'Add a couple zeroes on the end of my check?' Ha, ha, ha."

Mike of West St. Paul: "I know this is kind of stupid, in a way, but it was also kind of funny.

"The people from Miracle-Ear called up, and they said something about receiving information about their product.

"I said: 'What?' "

Jay of Hastings: "I work for a company that is in the hearing-aid business. EVERY TIME someone asks what kind of work I do, and I reply that I work with hearing aids, they reply: 'What?' Makes me want to hurl."

Dean of Eagan: "I work for a computer-consultant firm, so frequently I'm at the clients' sites. I usually end up sitting at the desk of someone who's out for the day—and invariably someone will walk up and say something stupid, like 'My, Cindy, how you've changed!' or 'Hello, Mary! I really like how you've done your hair!' "

Matt of Oakdale: "I work for a beer distributor, and anyone who's ever delivered beer or liquor or cases of lobster tail on a two-wheeler has heard this one from a bystander: 'You can just put that in the blue Chevy'—or brown Ford, or whatever they're driving. That's a real knee-slapper."

Navasanki of St. Paul: "I used to work as a parking-lot attendant at the University of Minnesota—at an outside lot, in the dead of winter. I worked from 5 in the morning until 10 in the morning; this was a miserable shift, and if I had a nickel for everyone who pulled up and said . . . 'Is it cold enough out for you?' I would be a wealthy, wealthy woman."

Michelle of St. Paul: "If I hear 'Workin' hard—or hardly workin'?' one more time, I swear to God I'm gonna slap somebody."

Dick of North St. Paul: "I'm a painter, and every single day, I hear: 'Oh, you missed a spot!' Or, even better yet: 'When you get done here, come over to my house.'

"I always tell 'em: 'Well, if I'm not there early, start without me.' "

Mr. T. of White Bear Lake: "When the home-shopping network first came on, they'd get on the phone and say: 'Hello! Can we help you?' And we used to say: 'Well, no. We're just browsing.' I don't think they really liked that."

"Karl" of Inver Grove Heights: "Me and my friends, like, find fun in going to them stores that say everything's a dollar? And asking the salespeople, like, how much it is? Even though we already know, like, it's a dollar? 'Cause everything in the store's a dollar?"

BULLETIN BOARD REPLIES: Like, cut it out?

That's a sentiment echoed, unquestionably, by **Lise** of Eau Claire, Wis.: "I happen to work in one of those dollar stores, and that's just the *beginning* of dollar-store customer jokes. People ask if the phone is a dollar, if the register is a dollar, if *we're* a dollar. It's just horrible."

Bob of Byerly's (a Twin Cities grocery chain): "I get my display all put up, and somebody comes up and asks: 'What if I want the bottom one?' I *hate* when they do that."

Jeff of St. Peter: "I'm a motel desk clerk in Mankato, and right at the check-in desk, it says: 'No Pets Allowed.' I work the graveyard shift, so I get the after-bar crowd—and it's normal to have a guy and his 'partner' show up (female, sometimes), and they'll be drunk, and one will nudge the other and say: 'Looks like you've gotta stay in the car.' "

L.B. of Lakeville: "I'm a flight attendant, and when two men who are obviously friends or business associates are boarding the plane together, the first one always says: 'My dad here has the boarding passes.' . . . I always laugh politely, like I've been doing for the past 12 years.

"I'd just like to mention this: It's always *men* who make these jokes; I've *never* had women make them."

Red of Oakdale: "A man will come up to the cash register with Midol, presumably for his wife, and he'll be holding his stomach and saying: 'Oh, the pain, the pain.' "

C.J. of Maplewood: "When my grandpa went to give blood, he'd ask whoever was taking the blood if he could play the piano after he was done. They'd say: 'Sure.' And he'd say: 'Good! Because I've always wanted to know how to play the piano.' "

G.C. of St. Paul ("who never eats in company-owned cafeterias"): "During college, I worked summers in a company-owned cafeteria, so not only did I hear the same Dumb Customer Jokes all the time, I heard them from the same dumb customers. (I learned I wasn't cut out for the service industry. Not only wasn't the customer always right, he—and it was usually a 'he'—was often a jerk.)

"Several customers just cracked themselves up with this 'joke': There is a long line of people waiting to be served; someone orders one of the day's specials; the next customer walks up and says: 'I'll have the same.' Most of it is already on their plate when they say something like: 'Except I'll have ham instead of beef, french fries instead of mashed potatoes, and peas instead of carrots.'

"Of course, the joke was on them. None of the food was fit for human consumption."

Carrie of Little Canada: "I've been working in a bar in Vadnais Heights for about four years. The most common drinks are the meat-and-potatoes drinks: a Windsor Coke, a Bacardi Coke, the beers.

"Whenever you tell them the price of the drink—i.e., $2.15, $2.30—they look at you, look at their watch and say, 'No it's not. It's 10:30!'

"I've been serving these people for four years. These same people tell me the same joke *every damn weekend!*"

Janet of St. Paul: "I'm a bartender. People are always ordering screwdrivers, and then they say: 'Gotta have my vitamin C.' And then, with an open bar where they don't have to pay, you'll get a couple of guys there, and the one'll say: 'Ha, ha. Put his drink on *my* tab!' And then you'll have a couple of middle-aged men, and the one man'll always say about the other: 'Oh, go check his I.D.' And then they'll laugh."

Bob of Bloomington: "I'm a bartender—and usually this happens when I'm busy, waiting on somebody. Somebody else walks in, and they don't want to wait, and they think we're just talking. They'll yell down to the side where I'm tending bar: 'Hey! Good place to open a bar here, wouldn't it?'

"Usually what I say is: 'Yes, but we're still waiting for our license.' What I really would like to say is: 'If you need anything, just shake your head. I'll hear you.'"

S.P. of Cottage Grove: "I'm a hairstylist, and nine out of 10 men, when you sit 'em down in your chair and ask 'How would you like you hair cut today?' they look with a real serious look on their face and say: 'Shorter.' And then they bust out laughin'. And I go: Oh, ho-ho-ho-ho. Oh, slap my knee— and then I say: 'No, seriously, how did you want your hair cut?' And they say it again: 'Shorter.'

"I hear that every day—and every time I hear it, I pretend like it's the first time, because we need those customers."

Uncle Mike of Eau Claire, Wis.: "I've got this big, round bald spot on top of my head, see, so whenever I go get my hair cut and I'm sitting in the chair, the stylist always says: 'So what would you like done?' And I always say: 'Well, cut off the back, trim the sides—and glue it right on top.' They always laugh, but now I think they're just patronizing me. I'm not sure."

Linda of Prescott, Wis.: "My hairdresser, Julie, is familiar with how I like my hair cut and styled, so I said: 'Just make me beautiful.' Then I wondered how many times she's heard that one. She replied: 'No problem.' What a gal."

Anonymous woman of Hutchinson: "A friend and I went to a grocery store in town here, and the checkout girl's name was Rhonda. My friend said: 'Ho, well! Help me, Rhonda. Help, help me, Rhonda.'

"This girl got a look on her face like 'I can't believe this.'

"My friend said: 'I bet you've heard *that* a few times!'"

"The girl just looked so bored."

Kelly of Woodbury: "I used to work at the Maplewood Rainbow Foods, as a cashier. Every time they ran the rerun of the 'Cheers' with Woody singing his song to his girlfriend, Kelly, for her birthday, people would come up to me: 'Oh! Your name's Kelly? You ever heard of "Kelly Kelly Kelly Kelly Kelly Kelly Kelly" '—and on and on and on; they'd sing the whole song to me.

"I'd laugh; I'd smile; I'd turn red . . ."

Jeanne of St. Paul: "The postmaster sometimes gets a customer who comes in and says: 'I need to buy the Grace Kelly stamps.' And you say: 'Well, why do you need that particular stamp?' And they'll say: 'Because I'm paying my bills during the . . . grace period.' "

Rogers of South St. Paul: "I'm a mailman, and I have a quiet neighborhood route. Oftentimes, people wait for me at their doors for their mail. Whenever I give someone a return-to-sender letter, they start singing that stupid song from the '60s. I've been doing routes for 20 years, and I must've heard it thousands of times."

BULLETIN BOARD REPLIES: Need we speculate on the potential connection between disgruntled postal workers and Dumb Customer Jokes?

Greg of the Eastern Heights, with a Dumb Tourist Joke: "About 10 years ago, I was in London, on the bridge that's right by the Tower of London, and there was a Beefeater standing there. I walked up to him and asked if I could have my picture taken with him. He looked at me and said: 'What a *novel* idea.' I felt about one inch high."

Erin of St. Paul, with another: "I was vacationing in Palm Springs. I happened to be eating at Sonny Bono's restaurant, and I had to do it; I knew that it was ridiculous, but I had to do it: He was there, and I had to say: 'I got you, babe.' "

BULLETIN BOARD REPLIES: Our Dept. of Ugly Americanism reports that a visitor from Minnesota walked into Rick's Cafe Americain in Casablanca a few years ago and, noticing a piano, walked over and plunked out the first verse of "As Time Goes By." Pleased with himself, he looked up to see the bored expression of the bartender, who deadpanned: "First time we've heard that in here."

Vince of Lilydale, with a Dumb Righthander Joke: "Just as bad as a Dumb Customer Joke: I golf lefthanded, and whenever I'm paired up with a new foursome, invariably someone will say, 'You're standing on the wrong side of the ball.' "

Sean of North St. Paul: "I work at a golf course, and part of my job is repairing irrigation breaks. *Every time* I'm out there digging to expose the pipe, I get a golfer who walks by and says: 'What—are ya diggin' for worms?'

"I tell you: It's enough to drive you nuts."

Elaine of White Bear, with a Dumb Passerby Joke: "I have never, ever washed my car out in my driveway without someone coming along and saying: 'Want to do mine next?' "

Jennifer of Burnsville, with another: "When my husband and I were living in Utah, we were laying about 6,000 square feet of sod—and I cannot tell you the number of cars that drove by and they rolled down the window and yelled: 'Green side up!' Ha, ha."

Cindy of Woodbury: "My brother-in-law, Marty, is a carpet installer, and people are always saying to him: 'Be sure to put it right side up.' Ha, ha, ha. The other thing they say is: As he's carrying in the pad that goes under the carpet, they say: 'Oh! That's not the color I ordered.' But the thing about that is: Most of those people are serious."

Kent of St. Paul: "I'm a professional carpet layer. On large jobs, such as office buildings, we frequently bring the entire roll of carpet out and cut it in the parking lot. Everybody thinks they're being so original when they come up to us and say: 'Ohhh! Carpeting the parking lot, eh?' "

C.M. of South St. Paul: "All summer long, I've been borrowin' my roommate's grandmother's lawn mower. She lives about three blocks away, and each day I borrow it, I have to roll it down the street. Every time I roll it down the street, I have these dumb neighbors that stick their head out the windows when they're driving by, and they say: 'Hey, you're supposed to be mowing the lawn, not the street.' "

Dave of St. Paul: "I'm a carpenter, and it never fails: When we're working up on ladders on a house, either a builder or a homeowner or some other tradesman will come around and say: 'Oh, movin' up in the world now, eh?' "

Charlie of Chippewa Falls, Wis.: "My dad played a bass violin in dance bands and orchestras in New York City in the 1930s. One time, he got on an elevator with his bass violin. The elevator operator asked him if he stuck that under his chin when he played it.

"My dad answered him, 'I suppose your work has its ups and downs.' "

Fuddy-duddy Buddy of White Bear Lake: "In the '50s, some passenger elevators had been converted to automatic operation, but many were still run by elevator operators. Uniforms were uniform. The buildings with large banks of elevators . . . even had 'starters' on the ground floor whose job was to ensure efficient operation by waiting until cars were full before allowing the operators to start. Some of them used castanets to signal an OK.

"One day in the Minneapolis telephone building, I stepped into a car, and as we proceeded upward, with originality, I commented to the operator: 'I suppose you have your ups and downs on this job.' She said: 'Yes—but it's the jerks that bother me.' Is that a true comeuppance?"

Michelle of Forest Lake, reporting from the Valleyfair amusement park: "On their Wild Rails ride, they have an attendant at the beginning who warns you: 'There will be an abrupt stop and a jerk at the end of the ride.' And then at the end of the ride, everybody gleefully choruses to the attendant: 'Hi, are you the jerk at the end of the ride?'

"They always groan. I think they're pretty good sports to put up with that."

Groundhog of Stillwater: "You guys are always talking about Dumb Customer Jokes; well, I've got Dumb Neighborhood Jokes.

"I just started driver's ed here in Stillwater, and every time I tell a neighbor about it, they're, like: 'You just tell me when you get behind the wheel, so I can pull the kids in, close the windows and lock all the doors.'

"Oh, silly people. I've heard that about 25 times since I started driver's ed."
BULLETIN BOARD REPLIES: What makes you think that's a joke?

Patient of Spooner, Wis., with a Dumb Dentist Joke: "I was at the dentist the other day getting a temporary crown put in. It must have been in a tough spot. He said: 'I'd give my right arm to be ambidextrous.'"

Doctor Friendly, with a Dumb Doctor Joke: "Not too long ago, I attended the delivery of the first baby born to a delightful black couple. After all the shouting was over, both literally and figuratively, I was chatting with them about the usual new-baby stuff—guessing the weight, seeing who he looked like, and so forth. I asked what they were going to name him, and was quite stunned at the obviously sincere answer: Sean Patrick So-and-so.

"Thinking myself pretty clever, I responded, 'That's funny. He doesn't look Irish.'

"Icy stares and deathly silence filled the room.

"Oh, well. I guess brand-new parents aren't always *[BULLETIN BOARD NOTES: or ever]* in the mood for jokes about their baby's name.

"At least the nurse thought it was funny."

Paul of St. Paul: "A little while ago, I had to avoid making a Dumb Customer Joke myself.

"I'm sittin' in the hospital right now, and my newborn baby son was just circumcised half an hour ago. *[BULLETIN BOARD NOTES: Sure. You can say "just."]* I was there watchin' it, and as the doctor was gettin' ready, they were layin' out the various instruments they have to use—and the last thing they laid out was this little shot glass, and they filled it up with this brown liquid.

"And I'm lookin' at it, and I'm lookin' at the doctor, and I'm lookin' at my baby, and it was all I could do not to ask him if the shot of booze was for him or the baby."

BULLETIN BOARD MUSES: The last thing you'd want is a doctor all tensed up, straining to hold that false smile, during a circumcision. Last thing we'd want, anyway.

Tracie of Highland Park: "I was out for lunch one day with my mom and sister, and we walked into a very obviously not-busy restaurant; there was one table with people sitting at it. And the manager comes over: 'Hi! Can I seat you?' And we said: 'Yeah. Table for three.'

"And my sister says to him: 'Well, you know, if you can fit us in, please do. But otherwise, I can see you're very busy and . . . oh, wait! I see a table way, way over in the corner! Do you think you could seat us there, or do you want us to sit down for a moment?'

"The manager looked at us, just blank. My sister said: 'It's a joke.' I told my sister: 'You just made a Dumb Customer Joke.'"

Tom of St. Paul, with a Dumb Skier Joke: "After I said to a lift operator, 'Well, it's all downhill from here,' my wife and I cringed for the rest of the day."

Brown of St. Paul: "Last weekend, I was at a hotel, and we were coming down to go to breakfast. And we get off the elevator, and in comes a waiter with room service—and I looked at him and I went: 'You can bring that to Room 928'—my room. And I was thinking: 'Oh, man, that was so *stupid!* It was a Dumb Customer Joke!'"

Nonstop Rock of Columbia Heights: "My friend and I both wear contact lenses. Whenever we go out for a few beers, the waiter will usually ask as they are delivering the bottles: 'Do you need glasses?' To which we simultaneously reply: 'No, we wear contacts.' This usually gets a genuine-sounding laugh, but now I wonder. Are we just two more Dumb Customers?"

Sue of Woodbury: "I did it. I'm embarrassed. I can't believe I did it—and it's your fault. I did a Dumb Customer Joke, and I only did it because you've planted these things in the back of my mind, and they manifest themselves when I'm at the store. And I blame you.

"I'll tell you what it was: My sister and I were at the grocery store; I was behind her in the checkout lane. She gets to the end of her groceries, and I said to the clerk: 'Oh, just add mine with hers.' And I laughed and laughed, and the clerk just kept punching her numbers. My sister glared at me and said: 'You did it.' I said: 'I know. . .'"

Jeff of St. Paul: "Until the Bulletin Board corrected me, I probably had the Dumbest Customer Joke in the world. Any time a clerk would come up to me in a store and say, 'May I help you, please,' I'd always say: 'No, I'm just shoplifting.' And they'd laugh: 'Ha, ha.' I don't do that anymore."

John J. Trammell of Shoreview: "I was getting my driver's license renewed Thursday morning, and after all the paperwork had been processed, my eyes checked, my new picture taken, I had to pay $15 for the renewal. I wrote out the check, and almost bit my tongue to keep from asking the clerk if she needed to see my driver's license. It was touch-and-go for a moment."

Doob of Roseville: "A Dumb Customer Joke was narrowly averted at Super-America this morning.

"My husband and I had a very romantic pizza supper after an orchestra concert last night, and I woke up feeling just a trifle bilious. Went over to Super-America and picked out at least three different strengths of antacid and anti-gas medicine. Got up to the counter and placed my purchases there and looked the guy in the eye, and he said: 'Do you have any gassssss-oline?' "

Mary of Stillwater, calling from Madison, Wis.: "I'm down here for a 20-year reunion with three of my high-school buddies. One of them is a colon/rectal surgeon now, and when we were chatting yesterday, I think I committed the cousin to the Dumb Customer Joke, which is the Dumb Friend Question.

"I had to ask her: 'How did you get into that?'

"She must have to field that question a lot, because she looked at me completely straight-faced and answered: 'Well, there was an opening.' Don't you think that's a good answer?"

A Faithful But Shy Reader of Rice Lake, Wis.: "I mentioned to the optometrist that my son had been studying for his eye exam all day. If looks could kill . . ."

Tom of St. Paul: "When I had my wisdom teeth taken out, I was watching the dentist set out his tools, and I asked him where the pliers were. He explained that they don't use pliers; they just pick around the tooth until it falls out. I could tell by his tone that I had said something stupid—something he'd heard a hundred times.

"My teeth didn't want to just fall out, and after a long, painful struggle, he finally excused himself and came back with a funny-looking set of pliers to finish the job.

"Score one for the Dumb Customers."

Patty of the Midway: "As a child-care provider, I'm a frequent visitor to the free and wonderful Como Zoo. On my latest excursion, it occurred to me that people are pretty humorous at the zoo. They howl outside the wolves' den and scratch their armpits outside the gorillas' cage, trying to get a rise out of these extremely bored animals.

"The gorillas' look says it all: 'Right, Bud. First time I've seen one of you guys do *that.*' "

R.N. of Eagan: "My husband and I went to the Science Museum in St. Paul. We went to see the mummy—and Mike said: That's what I look like when I wake up in the morning.

"And then this lady came up and said: 'Hey, kids! That's what I look like when I wake up in the morning!'

"I bet that mummy has heard a lot of Dumb Customer Jokes."

CHAPTER 22

The Kindness of Strangers

Reports of goodness in a world where goodness is unexpected:

The Kansan of Woodbury: "I was in the Group Health St. Paul clinic with my 2-year-old and my 1-year-old. I had three strikes against me: It was noon, and they were hungry, tired and bored. It's embarrassing and frustrating to have two fussy, demanding babies in public. This lovely white-haired lady began singing nursery rhymes to my little ones, and they fell into a peaceful trance—kind of like when they watch Barney. I was able to get my prescription and leave the clinic with a bit of sanity intact.

"We'd all be happier if grandmas were always around to sing us songs when we're cranky. Thank you, ma'am."

Donna of Lake Osakis, who ended with her voice trembling, fighting off tears: "I would like to thank whoever turned in a $100 personal check that my daughter Chris lost. She's a single, working mother and lost the check while getting gas on her way to work the other morning. That was the only money she had—and she was desperate.

"God bless the person who turned the check in to the Lexington City Hall. It just helped me restore my faith that, despite listening to the news and reading the newspaper, there's so many good people that nobody even mentions, you know. This is . . . really . . . I mean, my daughter's trying to make it, you know, and . . . this really . . . she got the money back, you know, and . . . I'd like to thank whoever turned the money back in."

Ex-welfare Dependent of West St. Paul: "Two years ago, I was forced to make a long trip from Minnesota to southern Illinois, and I had been saving as much as possible from my welfare checks to make the trip.

"Sometime during my return trip to Minnesota, my wallet—containing

168

the 30 bucks I had left to my name—fell out on the seat. Somebody took advantage of the situation, cleaned out the cash and dropped the wallet on the floor under the seat. When I left the train, I realized it was missing, so I retraced my steps and eventually found my wallet.

"A man who had seen me searching asked if I had a problem. I told him that someone had taken my money and I was angry, but I'd be OK. He opened his wallet, pulled out a bill, put it in my hand and said: 'This should pay for your cab home.'

"I just assumed that it was $5 or $10—and as he moved away into the crowd, I looked down to see if it really would be enough to get a cab. My eyes just about popped out of my skull when I saw it was a $100 bill—so I chased the man down, assuming he meant to give me 10 bucks. He insisted that I keep the money and that I put it away immediately, before I got myself mugged.

"I really just want to say thanks to that man. I didn't catch a cab that day, but that money bought me food for a month and kept my landlady from kicking me out. I'd like to pay him back, but I'm sure I'd have 20,000 people claiming that they were the one who had given me the hundred bucks, so instead, I've decided to pass the favor along to somebody else in need."

Jo of Hastings: "Left my purse on top of my car. Drove away. Everybody's honking, pointing at the top of my car. I'm totally ignoring 'em, waving at them.

"I go home, and this man is following me in his car. He'd picked up my purse, and he explained to me that if I wanted to go back and get the pennies, I could, but he'd picked up all the silver he could."

Goddess of St. Paul: "Purple and white rods were covering my head as Bonnie swiveled my chair to do the final wrapping of my perm. Out the window and across the street, at the Swede Hollow foreign-used-car dealership, in place under the shiny aqua fringes flapping in the breeze, were two white plastic lawn chairs sitting on the corner.

" 'What?' I said. 'Do people need to rest while they're looking at cars?'

" 'No,' said Bonnie, 'the owner felt sorry for the old ladies standing and waiting for the bus, so every day he brings out these two plastic chairs. Sometimes, in a gust of wind, because they are so lightweight, they tumble down the sidewalk, and he has to go after them. But that doesn't discourage him. He just puts them back in place, so they can sit. Eric is really a nice man.'

"After the hair thing, I went to Carson Pirie Scott at Rosedale. In the full-bodied beautiful woman's section was a tall, stunning African woman in a blue-and-white, full flowered dress, with a colorful turban on her head, carrying a golden purse. She looked like an African vision, and she and her friend were speaking in a foreign tongue.

"I went about my browsing, and around 10 minutes later, I noticed a bracelet lying on the carpet. It was about an inch wide and had interlocking links. There were small, square, lavender stones down the middle and small, round, pale-blue stones down one side and small, round, soft-coral-colored stones down the other.

"The clasp had come undone. I wrapped it around my wrist, and it fit perfectly. Should I turn it in? For all I knew, the shopper who lost it was long gone—and who would know where a bracelet was lost, anyway?

"However, this bracelet was so unusual that I knew it didn't come from around here. The stunning African woman was sitting in a chair waiting for her friend, who was trying on clothes. I walked across the corridor and asked: 'Did you lose a bracelet?'

"She looked at her bare arm and said: 'Why yes, I did!'

" 'Is this yours?' I said.

" 'Why yes, it is!'

"I am so glad I squelched that tiny voice that said 'Finders keepers, losers weepers' and followed my intuition instead.

"In part, this perhaps repays when I was driving down Nicollet Avenue in a drizzle. There was a black woman sitting on a bench, waiting for a light. She kept pointing, pointing to my car. My dashboard was lit up, so I didn't know what she meant. She finally got up and came over to say: 'Your lights are on dim.'

"I was touched that a black woman waiting in the rain would care about a white woman's safety in her car.

"What goes around comes around."

Marty of Woodbury: "We had a white rabbit in a fenced backyard in Woodbury for about four years—a dwarf rabbit. The rabbit ran free in the fenced yard.

"Just a week ago, it met an untimely death.

"Over those four years, the rabbit became a favorite of probably several hundred people who would stop with their children and look at it and have a marvelous time petting the rabbit.

"So after the rabbit died, in order to notify the people, I put a little cross out by the fence, with the birth and death dates. Over the next couple days, a couple different people—besides stopping and looking and asking questions, wondering about what happened to the rabbit—also left flowers. Tears came to my eyes."

Anonymous woman: "Twenty-three years ago, my dad died. Before he died, our TV was in the repair shop—and when the TV repairman delivered it, he must have found out that my dad died, because he had this puppy in his truck.

"He knew that me and my mom were alone then, and he says: 'Oh, yeah, someone left this little puppy in my truck.' Well, we fell in love with it, and then he said that we could have it—but he knew all along. It wasn't that somebody had left it in there; his plan was to give us this little puppy, to keep us company.

"We asked what the little puppy's name was; it turned out the dog was a girl, and the repairman's name was George. We ended up calling her Georgie Girl.

"I was only 15 at the time. If you're out there, George the TV repairman, God bless you."

Mary of Shoreview: "When our club was having a meeting for dinner at Christmastime, at a north-suburban Polish restaurant and bar, I pulled into the parking lot with a trunkful of gifts. A pickup truck was directly in front of me, and he parked a couple of spaces away.

"I turned off the car, popped the trunk-open button—and as I reached for the door handle, I was startled to see a grisly-looking man directly outside the driver's door. In his mid-30s, plaid shirt, jeans, kind of a grisly-looking beard, no jacket—and it was *cold*. He was just standing there, looking at me.

"I hesitated—10,000 things are crossing my mind, of course; not another soul in sight—and I remember very vividly the decisive thought that surfaced. It was: Well, I can't just sit in the car all night. Yes, B. Boarders, I hear you; I know all the horrible things that happen—and yet I opened the door and said: 'Yes?'—like I was *waiting on him*, for heaven's sake.

"He says: 'Can I take something in for you?' I gaped at him, and I said: 'Pardon?' He grins and says: 'Well, you popped the trunk, so I figured you had stuff to carry.' And I just said: 'Well, how nice of you.'

"So he carried in this huge box of gifts, gives me a grin, and bellies up to the bar to greet all his friends. I know there are a lot of loonies out there, but I have this horrible disease of trusting the basic goodness of people.

"In the midst of all of these horrible headlines—the druggies and the rapists and the killings for no reason—there are still lots of good people out there. I'd say: a large majority. And I just don't think that we can let all of these societal terrorists make us forget that fact. God bless."

Rosemary for Remembrance tells of being in line at the grocery store "behind a man who had a beautiful bouquet of flowers—roses—and I said: 'You're surely going to make someone happy.'

"We were standing in this long line, and after I had checked out my groceries, this man was at the end of the line—with one rose for me. I thought that was one of the nicest unbidden kindnesses that I'd ever experienced."

Josiah's Mom of North St. Paul: "My simple pleasure is my little boy. Oh, he's beautiful! He's 2 months old, and I love everything about him. I thought my life was great before I had him, but it's complete now. I took this beautiful 2-month-old boy to Rainbow Foods in Maplewood, and right as I got to the checkout stand, he decided he needed to eat—immediately—and he let everybody in the store know about it. So I've got this frantic, crying little 2-month-old boy wanting to be nursed, and I had to bag up my groceries, and this lady across the aisle took pity on me and came and bagged my groceries for me. I just thought that was so wonderful.

"I haven't lost faith in humanity; I've got humanity in my arms."

Mama K. of Lino Lakes: "I was drivin' to work the other day, in the late afternoon. On the bicycle path next to me, there's a kid in his wheelchair. Another kid on his bicycle. The kid in the wheelchair is hangin' on to the bike seat; the other guy is givin' him a ride. Off they go. They're laughin', they're smilin', they're talkin', they're havin' a wonderful time.

"I don't know why, but it just grabbed me. By the time I got to the stop sign, tears were rollin' down my face. I thought: 'Yeah, well what's wrong with this world? Well damn, what's *right* with it!'

"A little brotherly love, a little friendship love. They're gonna be all right, this younger generation. This mama knows."

Judy of Woodbury: "I was reading about the woman whose child was lost at the Fair, and it reminded me of when we were there and we found a lost little girl named Stephanie. Her mother's name was Janet, and her dad's name was 'Daddy,' and she was from Virginia, Minnesota. Just the sweetest little child; 4 years old—and had a sister that was 'zero.'

"The nice thing that happened was: I was holding her and comforting her, and this guy walked by who had won three stuffed animals, and he said: 'Oh, would you like to pick one?' And so he gave her one—and I'll tell you: That did it for her. She was just fine."

J.S. of Highland Park: "We were at Como Zoo [in St. Paul] today. I'd picked up my 3-year-old daughter, and we met my son's class—he's in kindergarten—and we stayed after his class had gone. My son had really wanted one of these free gliders they were giving away, and I said: 'Just wait; your sister has to finish playing in the playground'—and by the time we got there, they were all gone. My son started crying—quite heartfeltedly. And this boy, who was only about 8 or 9, came up, out of the blue—he had seen Matt crying—and said: 'Here. Take mine.'

"It was so sweet. It was so wonderful. It was so generous."

L. of Stillwater: "I really think my boyfriend, J., is the most wonderful man. We have been together for almost eight years, and he never ceases to amaze me. I have to tell you about one incident that makes me especially proud:

"We were at Rosedale one night, and we went into Woolworth's. When we got up to the cash register, there was a little girl asking about the price of this gumball machine she had in her tiny hand. Apparently, it was too expensive, because she put it back and went back to her parents looking really sad.

"Well, J. was watching this pretty intently. He asked the cashier how much the gumball machine was, paid for it and then told the cashier to give it to the little girl after we left the store.

"So, we left the store, hid behind the escalator and watched this little girl. When the cashier gave her the gumball machine, she started just *squealing* and grinning. Her parents were smiling, and the cashier was shrugging her shoulders, and I was just about crying."

M.B. of the East Side: "Every winter, I'm reminded of one man's act of kindness—and I bless his name.

"I was headed east on 94 into Wisconsin, and I had just purchased two new snow tires—retreads. The wind chill was way below zero—*way* below— and the tread peeled right off one of the tires.

"It was so cold; I got out, and I had the regular tires in the trunk, but your hands became useless in seconds. And this man stopped, across the median strip, and he walked over and offered his assistance.

"He changed the tire—and suggested that I get off at the next exit and come back to St. Paul, because the other tire might do the same.

"So I was driving very slowly—and before I got to the next exit, the other one did the same thing. And this man, who had been watching to see if I made it, came back and changed the other tire.

"When I asked his name and address, to send him some money, he said: 'My thanks would be if someone would do the same for my wife someday.' Bless that man."

Gypsi of New Brighton, speaking of a *very* cold day in Minnesota: "Last Thursday afternoon, I spoke to my mother, and she was rushing off to a doctor's appointment. As she was driving down 94, her car broke down just before the Marion Street exit. Her car just stopped running.

"She pulled to the side, and she waited there; she put her hood up and waited there for at least a half-hour—maybe longer—and nobody stopped to help her. And as she's describing this to me later on, my heart's thumping—thinking of my mother, who's not in very good physical condition, stranded by herself on the freeway.

"She got out of the car and started walking to the Marion Street exit, and up the exit ramp; she has arthritis and angina pains, and my heart was racing as she was telling me this. She told me that a car pulled over, and it scared me to think of my mother possibly being accosted by somebody who's pulling over to *seemingly* help her.

"Well, in the car was a beautiful woman named Judy who had a little girl in the backseat—4 years old, named Crystal, who had a little friend named Tony living in her tummy. This woman gave my mother a ride—in the cold, cold winter—to Sears, and may have saved my mother from significant harm.

"I want to thank Judy and Crystal and little Tony, to say the least; thank you for taking care of my mother for me and watching over her, so she could be safe and warm and happy. She has little grandchildren who love her to death.

"Judy said the reason that she helped my mother was because nobody would help *her* mother when the same thing happened to her. Thank you, Judy—and I promise I will always stop to help someone when they need it. Thank you for your kindness and your love, because now I still have my mother."

Kathy of Marine: "My daughter works in Marine. It's about five miles from us, and sometimes she has to ride her bike to work if we can't give her a ride. Then we pick her up when she's done working.

"My husband was late picking her up one evening last week—she works 'til about 8:30—and she was mad, and she started to ride her bike home; she wasn't gonna wait for him. So she's riding along, mad, and he comes up behind her, following her route after he found that she'd left. And he's following her a little ways, because she's miffed and won't pay any attention to him.

"She finally stops; he stops; she puts her bike in the back of the truck; she gets in the truck. Meanwhile, a woman had passed him, and she started backing up and asked if everything was OK—because she'd seen him following Sarah. And I just thought that was really a risk to take, especially considering how things are today, and I just thought she should be applauded.

"It was brave of her—and really, if we all would do that more often, maybe we wouldn't have so many kids gone. So cheers to you, lady."

Larry of St. Paul: "I'm calling to tell you about a good deed that could quite possibly have run amok. I was traveling west on Highway 36, and I noticed a man whose car had stalled; he was walking with his child in his arms. Thinking that that simply would not do, I immediately began to pull over.

"Unfortunately, the person in front of me and the person in back of me both had the same idea. All three of us pulled over as one onto the shoulder, the guy in front of me slamming on his brakes, me going to the right of him, the person behind me going to the right of me, into the ditch. Knowing he couldn't stay there, he hit the accelerator, zoomed way ahead, got about a hundred yards ahead, out of trouble, back onto the shoulder. We paused, let our adrenal glands settle—and the two others took off.

"Me, having won the prize of being able to help the fellow, got out of my truck, walked back there. It turns out the guy is from New York City—and once I'd convinced him that I didn't want his wallet, he was agog. He couldn't believe that three people pulled over all at once to get him. He insisted on getting me something for my trouble. When we got to his house, he went in, came back out with a six-pack of foreign beer, handed it to me and said: 'Enjoy. Thank you very much.' Unfortunately, I don't drink—but I kept it anyway."

Randy Stokes of Apple Valley: "About 10 years ago, I lived in Washington State, where I struggled to eke out a living as a woodcrafter. I would drive down to Portland every weekend to participate in the local crafts market. It was a hard life, but particularly stressful during the Christmas season.

"Late one Sunday night near Christmas, my wife and I were driving home after a grueling weekend fighting rain, crowds and poor sales. It was about a two-hour drive, and we stopped at a small roadside cafe in Kelso, Washington, for some coffee. It was the model of a small-town café: nothing fancy, with a few locals and very little else.

"We must have looked like a mess when we dragged in. We were only planning on ordering coffee, since sales had been bad and we were nearly broke. But when the waitress came to take our order, she said: 'That man over there wants to buy you dinner.'

"We looked; the man at the counter was nursing a cup of coffee and looking the other way. Our bewilderment was evident, so the waitress repeated herself, then shrugged and said: 'He likes to do things like this at Christmas.'

"We were flustered, but he turned briefly and motioned for us to go ahead. So we thanked him as best we could and quickly scanned the menu for the cheapest thing we could find, like a tuna sandwich. 'No, no!' he cried. 'That won't do at all! You like steak?' He turned to the waitress and said: 'Two T-bone steaks, and whatever else they want.'

"He left the café only minutes later, while we were still trying to gather our wits. I have no idea who he was, but he has left us a Christmas memory that we will cherish in our hearts forever."

Mary Swank of St. Cloud: "I just thought I really should spread this wonderful Christmas story. It's all true; it just happened to me a week ago—and we're all still overwhelmed by it. The story begins:

"On Tuesday, December 14, an envelope arrived in my mailbox addressed to the Swank Family—but did not show a return address. I discovered three envelopes inside, all addressed to us.

"When I opened the first envelope, I discovered a sheaf of gift certificates for Target. The second envelope carried a similar amount of Cub Foods gift certificates. By this time, my seven children had formed a human drum roll around me as I prepared to open the third envelope—a Christmas card with a hand-written note, which we all ignored momentarily to find the signature at the bottom.

"*Nichts.* But what a note! Addressed to Casey, Mary and Kids, it said that though we don't know them, they feel a special kinship to us by virtue of having grown up in a large family such as the one my husband and I are raising. They'd decided among themselves that rather than exchange gifts this years, they'd rather share their gifts with us. Whoa.

"I won't disclose the amazing amount this gift tallied to, but suffice it to say that when I called my husband at work to proclaim the good news, he was only *slightly* less surprised than the day I called to tell him we were expecting twins—our sixth and seventh.

"Whoever and wherever you are, may I call you Santa? I want to tell you that because of your inspiration, I now give everyone a knowing wink. After all, this joyful giver could be *anyone.*

"My kids will remember this amazing gesture of generosity all their lives; their eyes were popping with disbelief. Who can say how many generations your act will affect?

"I'm truly filled with your gift—which, as with the old saint, has absolutely no strings attached. You didn't *owe* us, and you've made sure we won't owe you. A lot of the feelings of goodwill I now bear on my fellow humans are purely voluntary—all of the feelings. You have truly spread the genuine spirit of Christmas—all over the place. Thank you.

"That's my story. Isn't it . . . pretty cool?"

Distressed of St. Paul: "This is about what's wrong with people—and what's right with people. This has been on my mind since breakfast Sunday, and I had to tell someone about it:

"While having breakfast at one of the family restaurants in town, we were all disturbed by one family. The father was verbally and physically abusing a small boy.

"Why do people *do* that? The father was making more noise and fuss than the child.

"What is *wrong* is: We all just sat there and listened to this. I know what was going through *my* mind, and I'm sure it was similar to what other people were thinking: that it wasn't our place to involve ourselves with other people's domestic affairs. And, you know, what if this guy gets mad and punches us? Or what if he's armed?

"The last straw was when the father was taking the boy back from the rest room, and the little boy started to run ahead a little bit. The father grabbed the boy by the back of the shirt and lifted him up off the floor. Only his little toes were touching the floor. The father was propelling him forward and yelling at him for running, while the boy was desperately grabbing the front of his shirt, trying to pull it away from his neck—because he was being choked by his own shirt.

"We all just sat there, murmuring against this adult for what he was doing to this child—but murmur and shake with rage is all that we did.

"Finally, a gentle man stepped up and politely told the father that that was quite enough—and that he was choking the child. The father replied that he only had hold of the kid's shirt, that he wasn't choking him. And this gentle man explained how the child *was* being choked. The father let go of the child.

"We all sat there again—murmuring how good it was that this gentle man had said something, and how it was about time someone said something. We did a lot of good with our murmuring, didn't we?

"Well, after the people in the area around this family went back to eating and the family was quiet, that gentle man got up again and walked over and talked to the father. This man explained that he also had children and lived with a temper, and he talked about how much energy children have and how easy it is for them to get on your nerves, but often if you just give them a little positive attention, they soon settle down.

"Those of us around this table listened with reverence. Here was a man who knew the right words to say. The father was opening up and talking to this gentle stranger. The gentle man had touched the father on his shoulder, held his hand, showed him that even though he was a stranger, he cared. This gentle man told the father how important it is to talk about anger and find positive ways to release that anger.

"When the gentle man left, what a change there was in the father and mother of this little boy. The gentle man had gone over to talk to the father because he was worried that the father might retaliate against the boy for embarrassing him in the restaurant. The father was kinder to the boy, and as that gentle man left, a few of us thanked him.

"Why did we *thank* him? Why didn't any of the rest of us get up and do what *he* did? Even if he just kept that boy from getting one whipping, it was worth it. That gentle man may have made a permanent difference in this family's lives just by his caring and his few words.

"Was this gentle man different, or special? Was he a pastor or psychologist who had special training in counseling? Of course, he *must* be. But no, he was just a man; he was a father and a husband, and he had no special training to talk to people. He spoke from the heart, and it showed on his face.

"It wasn't an easy thing for him to do. When I was watching him write his check to pay his bill, his hands were trembling and he could hardly write. His face was pale. I was curious, and went up to him and asked why he did what the rest of us did not have the courage to do. And he said he did nothing more than anyone else would have done in the same case.

"How wrong he was. There was a whole roomful of people who just sat there and watched, and we didn't do a thing.

"God's blessings on that gentle man, and may we all strive to be more like him."

BILL ALKOFER

About the Editor

The voice of Bulletin Board—that mysterious "we" who listens to the calls and reads the letters—is Daniel Kelly, who created Bulletin Board in 1990 and has edited it since.

Almost everyone calls him Dan.

He is a native of Minnesota who graduated from Harvard College in 1975. Before coming to the *Saint Paul Pioneer Press*, he was editor of *Minnesota Monthly* and *Twin Cities* magazines.

He lives in Hopkins, Minn., with his wife and their two daughters.

How to Order
Pioneer Books

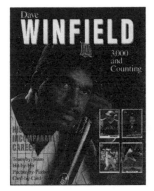

Dave Winfield: 3,000 and Counting . . .

This commemorative book, following Dave Winfield's career from childhood through his 3000th hit, is available for $9.95, plus postage and handling.

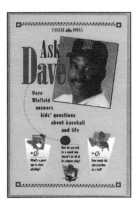

Ask Dave: Dave Winfield answers kids' questions about baseball and life.

This question-and-answer book is available for $7.95, plus postage and handling.

The Best of Bulletin Board

Enjoy these extraordinary stories told by ordinary folks, available for $8.95, plus postage and handling.

Call (800) 642-6480 to order.